Also by

MAYA ANGELOU

AUTOBIOGRAPHY

I Know Why the Caged Bird Sings
Gather Together in My Name
Singin' and Swingin' and Gettin' Merry Like Christmas
The Heart of a Woman
All God's Children Need Traveling Shoes
A Song Flung Up to Heaven

ESSAYS

Wouldn't Take Nothing for My Journey Now
Even the Stars Look Lonesome

POETRY

Just Give Me a Cool Drink of Water 'Fore I Diiie
Oh Pray My Wings are Gonna Fit Me Well
And Still I Rise
Shaker, Why Don't You Sing?
I Shall Not Be Moved
On the Pulse of Morning
Phenomenal Woman
The Complete Collected Poems of Maya Angelou
A Brave and Startling Truth
Amazing Peace
Mother
Celebrations

CHILDREN'S BOOKS

My Painted House, My Friendly Chicken, and Me
Kofi and His Magic

PICTURE BOOKS

Now Sheba Sings the Song
Life Doesn't Frighten Me

COOKERY

Hallelujah! The Welcome Table
Good Food, All Day Long

MOM & ME & MOM

M *u*

virago

VIRAGO

First published in Great Britain in 2013 by Virago Press

First published in the United States by Random House,
an imprint of The Random House Publishing Group, a
division of Random House Inc., New York

A CIP catalogue record for this book
is available from the British Library.

ISBN 978-1-84408-914-7

Printed and bound in Great Britain by
Clays Ltd, St Ives plc

Papers used by Virago are from well-managed forests
and other responsible sources.

MIX
Paper from
responsible sources
FSC
www.fsc.org **FSC® C104740**

Virago Press
An imprint of
Little, Brown Book Group
100 Victoria Embankment
London EC4Y 0DY

An Hachette UK Company
www.hachette.co.uk

www.virago.co.uk

I give particular thanks to Vivian Baxter,
who generously taught me how to be a mother,
allowing me to dedicate this book to one of
the most courageous and generous men I know,
my son, Guy Bailey Johnson.

PROLOGUE

Frequently, I have been asked how I got to be this way. How did I, born black in a white country, poor in a society where wealth is adored and sought after at all costs, female in an environment where only large ships and some engines are described favorably by using the female pronoun—how did I get to be Maya Angelou?

Many times I have wanted to quote Topsy, the young black girl in *Uncle Tom's Cabin*. I have been tempted to say, "I dunno. I just growed." I never used that response, for a number of reasons. First, because I read the book in my early teens and the ignorant black girl embarrassed me. Second, I knew that I had become the woman I am because of the grandmother I loved and the mother I came to adore.

Their love informed, educated, and liberated me. I lived with my paternal grandmother from the time I was three years old until I was thirteen. My grandmother never kissed me during those years. However, when she had company, she would summon me to stand in front of her visitors. Then she would stroke my arms asking, "Have you ever seen arms more beautiful, straight as a plank and brown as peanut butter?" Or she would give me a tablet and a pencil. She would call out numbers to me in front of her company.

"All right sister, put 242, then 380, then 174, then 419; now add that." She would speak to the visitors, "Now watch. Her uncle Willie has timed her. She can finish that in two minutes. Just wait."

When I told the answer, she would beam with pride. "See? My little professor."

Love heals. Heals and liberates. I use the word *love,* not meaning sentimentality, but a condition so strong that it may be that which holds the stars in their heavenly positions and that which causes the blood to flow orderly in our veins.

This book has been written to examine some of the ways love heals and helps a person to climb impossible heights and rise from immeasurable depths.

MOM
& ME

"My mother was to remain a startling beauty."

(1976)

1

The first decade of the twentieth century was not a great time to be born black and poor and female in St. Louis, Missouri, but Vivian Baxter was born black and poor, to black and poor parents. Later she would grow up and be called beautiful. As a grown woman she would be known as the butter-colored lady with the blowback hair.

Her father, a Trinidadian with a heavy Caribbean accent, had jumped from a banana boat in Tampa, Florida, and evaded immigration agents successfully all his life. He spoke often and loudly with pride at being an American citizen. No one explained to him that simply wanting to be a citizen was not enough to make him one.

Contrasting with her father's dark chocolate complexion, her mother was light-colored enough to pass for white. She was called an octoroon, meaning that she had one-eighth Negro blood. Her hair was long and straight. At the kitchen table, she amused her children by whirling her braids like ropes and then later sitting on them.

Although Vivian's mother's people were Irish, she had been raised by German adoptive parents, and she spoke with a decided German accent.

Vivian was the firstborn of the Baxter children. Her sister Leah was next, followed by brothers Tootie, Cladwell, Tommy, and Billy.

As they grew, their father made violence a part of their inheritance. He said often, "If you get in jail for theft or burglary, I will let you rot. But if you are charged with fighting, I will sell your mother to get your bail."

The family became known as the "Bad Baxters." If someone angered any of them, they would track the offender to his street or to his saloon. The brothers (armed) would enter the bar. They would station themselves at the door, at the ends of the bar, and at the toilets. Uncle Cladwell would grab a wooden chair and break it, handing Vivian a piece of the chair.

He would say, "Vivian, go kick that bastard's ass."

Vivian would ask, "Which one?"

Then she would take the wooden weapon and use it to beat the offender.

When her brothers said, "That's enough," the Baxter gang would gather their violence and quit the scene, leaving their mean reputation in the air. At home they told their fighting stories often and with great relish.

Grandmother Baxter played piano in the Baptist church and she liked to hear her children sing spiritual gospel songs. She would fill a cooler with Budweiser and stack bricks of ice cream in the refrigerator.

The same rough Baxter men led by their fierce older sister would harmonize in the kitchen on "Jesus Keep Me Near the Cross":

> *There a precious fountain*
> *Free to all, a healing stream,*
> *Flows from Calvary's mountain.*

The Baxters were proud of their ability to sing. Uncle Tommy and Uncle Tootie had bass voices; Uncle Cladwell, Uncle Ira, and Uncle Billy were tenors; Vivian sang alto; and Aunt Leah sang a high soprano (the family said she also had a sweet tremolo). Many years later, I heard them often, when my father, Bailey Johnson Sr., took me and my brother, called Junior, to stay with the Baxters in St. Louis. They were proud to be loud and on key. Neighbors often dropped in and joined the songfest, each trying to sing loudest.

Vivian's father always wanted to hear about the rough games his sons played. He would listen eagerly, but if their games ended without a fight or at least a scuffle, he would blow air through his teeth and say, "That's little boys' play. Don't waste my time with silly tales."

Then he would tell Vivian, "Bibbi, these boys are too big to play little girls' games. Don't let them grow up to be women."

Vivian took his instruction seriously. She promised her father she would make sure they were tough. She led her brothers to the local park and made them watch as she climbed the highest tree. She picked fights with the toughest boys in her neighborhood, never asking her brothers to help, counting on them to wade into the fight without being asked.

Her father chastised her when she called her sister a sissy.

He said, "She's just a girl, but you are more than that. Bibbi, you are Papa's little girl-boy. You won't have to be so tough forever. When Cladwell gets up some size, he will take over."

Vivian said, "If I let him."

Everyone laughed, and recounted the escapades about when Vivian taught them how to be tough.

2

My mother, who was to remain a startling beauty, met my father, a handsome soldier, in 1924. Bailey Johnson had returned from World War I with officer's honors and a fake French accent. They were unable to restrain themselves. They fell in love while Vivian's brothers walked around him threateningly. He had been to war, and he was from the South, where a black man learned early that he had to stand up to threats, or else he wasn't a man.

The Baxter boys could not intimidate Bailey Johnson, especially after Vivian told them to lay off, to straighten up, and fly right. Vivian's parents were not happy that she was marrying a man from the South who was neither a doctor nor lawyer. He said he was a dietitian. The Baxters said that meant he was just a Negro cook.

Vivian and Bailey left the contentious Baxter atmosphere and moved to California, where little Bailey was born. I came along two years later. My parents soon proved to each other that they couldn't stay together. They were matches and gasoline. They even argued about how they were to break up. Neither wanted the responsibility of taking care of two toddlers. They separated and sent me and Bailey to my father's mother in Arkansas.

I was three and Bailey was five when we arrived in Stamps, Arkansas. We had identification tags on our arms and no adult supervision. I learned later that Pullman car porters and dining car waiters were known to take children off trains in the North and put them on other trains heading south.

Save for one horrific visit to St. Louis, we lived with my father's mother, Grandmother Annie Henderson, and her other son, Uncle Willie, in Stamps until I was thirteen. The visit to St. Louis lasted only a short time but I was raped there and the rapist had been killed. I thought I had caused his death because I told his name to the family. Out of guilt, I stopped talking to everyone except Bailey. I decided that my voice was so powerful that it could kill people, but it could not harm my brother because we loved each other so much.

My mother and her family tried to woo me away

from mutism but they didn't know what I knew: that my voice was a killing machine. They soon wearied of the sullen, silent child and sent us back to Grandmother Henderson in Arkansas, where we lived quietly and smoothly within my grandmother's care and under my uncle's watchful eye.

When my brilliant brother Bailey was fourteen he had reached a dangerous age for a black boy in the segregated South. It was a time when if a white person walked down the one paved block in town, any Negro on the street had to step aside and walk in the gutter.

Bailey would obey the unspoken order but sometimes he would sweep his arm theatrically and loudly say, "Yes, sir, you are the boss, boss."

Some neighbors saw how Bailey acted in front of white folks downtown and reported to Grandmother.

She called us both over and said to Bailey, "Junior"—her nickname for him—"you been downtown showing out? Don't you know these white folks will kill you for poking fun of them?"

"Momma"—my brother and I often called her that—"all I do is get off the street they are walking on. That's what they want, isn't it?"

"Junior, don't play smart with me. I knew the time would come when you would grow too old for the South. I just didn't expect it so soon. I will write to your mother and daddy. You and Maya, and especially you, Bailey, will have to go back to California, and soon."

Bailey jumped up and kissed Grandmother. He said, "I'm Brer Rabbit in the briar patch."

Even Grandmother had to laugh. The folktale told how a farmer whose carrots the rabbit had been stealing caught Brer Rabbit. The farmer threatened to kill the rabbit and turn him into a stew. The rabbit said, "I deserve that, please kill me, just don't throw me in that briar patch, please sir, anything but that, anything."

The farmer asked, "You're afraid of the briar patch?"

Rabbit, shaking and trembling, said, "Yes, sir, please kill me and eat me, just don't throw me . . . "

The farmer grabbed the rabbit by its long ears and threw him into a stand of weeds.

Rabbit jumped up and down. "That's where I wanted to be all along!"

I knew Bailey wanted to be reunited with his mother, but I was very comfortable with Grandmother Henderson. I loved her and I liked her and I felt safe under the umbrella of her love. I knew that for Bailey's sake we had to go back to California. Black boys his age who even noticed white girls risked being beaten, bruised, or lynched by the Ku

Klux Klan. He had not yet mentioned a white girl, but as he was growing into his manhood, seeing a pretty white girl and being moved by her beauty was inevitable.

I said, "Yes, I'm ready to go."

"I am Lady, and still your mother."

(Stockton, California, 1976)

3

My grandmother made arrangements with two Pullman car porters and a dining car waiter for tickets for herself, my brother, and me. She said she and I would go to California first and Bailey would follow a month later. She said she didn't want to leave me without adult supervision, because I was a thirteen-year-old girl. Bailey would be safe with Uncle Willie. Bailey thought he was looking after Uncle Willie, but the truth was, Uncle Willie was looking after him.

By the time the train reached California, I had become too frightened to accept the idea that I was going to meet my mother at last.

My grandmother took my hands. "Sister, there is nothing to be scared for. She is your mother, that's all. We are not surprising her. When she received my letter explaining how Junior was growing up, she invited us to come to California."

Grandmother rocked me in her arms and

hummed. I calmed down. When we descended the train steps, I looked for someone who could be my mother. When I heard my grandmother's voice call out, I followed the voice and I knew she had made a mistake, but the pretty little woman with red lips and high heels came running to my grandmother.

"Mother Annie! Mother Annie!"

Grandmother opened her arms and embraced the woman. When Momma's arms fell, the woman asked, "Where is my baby?"

She looked around and saw me. I wanted to sink into the ground. I wasn't pretty or even cute. That woman who looked like a movie star deserved a better-looking daughter than me. I knew it and was sure she would know it as soon as she saw me.

"Maya, Marguerite, my baby." Suddenly I was wrapped in her arms and in her perfume. She pushed away and looked at me. "Oh baby, you're beautiful and so tall. You look like your daddy and me. I'm so glad to see you."

She kissed me. I had not received one kiss in all the years in Arkansas. Often my grandmother would call me and show me off to her visitors. "This is my grandbaby." She would stroke me and smile. That was the closest I had come to being kissed. Now Vivian Baxter was kissing my cheeks and my lips and my hands. Since I didn't know what to do, I did nothing.

Her home, which was a boardinghouse, was filled with heavy and very uncomfortable furniture. She showed me a room and said it was mine. I told her I wanted to sleep with Momma. Vivian said, "I suppose you slept with your grandmother in Stamps, but she will be going home soon and you need to get used to sleeping in your own room."

My grandmother stayed in California, watching me and everything that happened around me. And when she decided that everything was all right, she was happy. I was not. She began to talk about going home, and wondering aloud how her crippled son was getting along. I was afraid to let her leave me, but she said, "You are with your mother now and your brother will be coming soon. Trust me, but more than that trust the Lord. He will look after you."

Grandmother smiled when my mother played jazz and blues very loudly on her record player. Sometimes she would dance just because she felt like it, alone, by herself, in the middle of the floor. While Grandmother accepted behavior so different, I just couldn't get used to it.

My mother watched me without saying much for about two weeks. Then we had what was to become familiar as "a sit-down talk-to."

She said, "Maya, you disapprove of me because I am not like your grandmother. That's true. I am not. But I am your mother and I am working some part of my anatomy off to pay for this roof over your head. When you go to school, the teacher will smile at you and you will smile back. Students you don't even know will smile and you will smile. But on the other hand, I am your mother. If you can force one smile on your face for strangers, do it for me. I promise you I will appreciate it."

She put her hand on my cheek and smiled. "Come on, baby, smile for Mother. Come on. Be charitable."

She made a funny face and against my will, I smiled. She kissed me on my lips and started to cry. "That's the first time I have seen you smile. It is a beautiful smile. Mother's beautiful daughter can smile."

I was not used to being called beautiful.

That day, I learned that I could be a giver simply by bringing a smile to another person. The ensuing years have taught me that a kind word or a vote of support can be a charitable gift. I can move over and make another place for another to sit. I can turn my music up if it pleases, or down if it is annoying.

I may never be known as a philanthropist, but I certainly want to be known as charitable.

———

I was beginning to appreciate her. I liked to hear her laugh because I noticed that she never laughed at anyone. After a few weeks it became clear that I was not using any title when I spoke to her. In fact, I rarely started conversations. Most often, I simply responded when I was spoken to.

She asked me into her room. She sat on her bed and didn't invite me to join her.

"Maya, I am your mother. Despite the fact that I left you for years, I am your mother. You know that, don't you?"

I said, "Yes, ma'am." I had been answering her briefly with a few words since my arrival in California.

"You don't have to say 'ma'am' to me. You're not in Arkansas."

"No, ma'am. I mean no."

"You don't want to call me 'Mother,' do you?"

I remained silent.

"You have to call me something. We can't go through life without you addressing me. What would you like to call me?"

I had been thinking of that since I first saw her. I said, "Lady."

"What?"

"Lady."

"Why?"

"Because you are beautiful, and you don't look like a mother."

"Is Lady a person you like?"

I didn't answer.

"Is Lady a person you might learn to like?"

She waited as I thought about it.

I said, "Yes."

"Well, that's it. I am Lady, and still your mother."

"Yes, ma'am. I mean yes."

"At the right time I will introduce my new name."

She left me, turned up the player, and sang loudly with the music. The next day I realized she must have spoken to my grandmother.

Grandmother came into my bedroom. "Sister, she is your mother and she does care for you."

I said, "I'll wait until Bailey gets here. He will know what to do, and whether we should call her Lady."

4

Mother, Grandmother, and I waited at the railway station. Bailey descended from the train and saw me first. The smile that took over his face made me forget all the discomfort I had felt since coming to California.

His eyes found Grandmother and his smile changed to a grin, and he waved to her. Then he saw Mother and his response broke my heart. Suddenly he was a lost little boy who had been found at last. He saw his mother, his home, and then all his lonely birthdays were gone. His nights when scary things made noise under the bed were forgotten. He went to her as if hypnotized. She opened her arms and she clasped him into her embrace. I felt as if I had stopped breathing. My brother was gone, and he would never come back.

He had forgotten everything, but I remembered how we felt on the few occasions when she sent us toys. I poked the eyes out of each doll, and Bailey took huge rocks and smashed to bits the trucks or trains that came wrapped up in fancy paper.

Grandmother put her arm around me and we walked ahead of the others back to the car. She opened the door and sat in the backseat. She looked at me and patted the seat beside her. We left the front seat for the new lovers.

The plan was that Grandmother would return to Arkansas two days after Bailey arrived. Before Lady and Bailey Jr. reached the car I said to Grandmother, "I want to go back home with you, Momma."

She asked, "Why?"

I said, "I don't want to think of you on that train all alone. You will need me."

"When did you make that decision?" I didn't want to answer.

She said, "When you saw the reunion of your brother and his mother?" That she should have such understanding, being an old woman and country, too: I thought it was amazing. It was just as well that I had no answer, because Bailey and his mother had already reached the car.

Vivian said to Grandmother, "Mother Annie, I didn't look for you two. I knew you would go to the car." Bailey didn't turn to look at me. His eyes were glued to his mother's face. "One thing about you that cannot be denied, you are a true sensible woman."

Grandmother said, "Thank you, Vivian. Junior?"

She had to call twice to get his attention, "Junior, how was the train? Did somebody make food for your trip? How did you leave Willie?"

Suddenly he remembered there was someone else in the world. He grinned for Grandmother. "Yes, ma'am, but none of them can cook like you."

He turned to me and asked, "What's happening, My? Has California got your tongue? You haven't said a word since I got in the car."

I made my voice as cold as possible. I said, "You haven't given me a chance."

In a second he said, "What's the matter, My?"

I had hurt him and I was glad. I said, "I may go back to Stamps with Momma." I wanted to break his heart.

"No, ma'am, you will not." My grandmother's voice was unusually hard.

My mother asked, "Why would you leave now? You said all you were waiting on was your brother. Well, here he is." She started the car and pulled out into traffic.

Bailey turned back to her. He added, "Yep, I'm in California."

19

Grandmother held my hand and patted it. I bit the inside of my mouth to keep from crying.

No one spoke until we reached our house. Bailey dropped his hand over the back of the front seat. When he wiggled his fingers, I grabbed them. He squeezed my fingers and let them go and drew his hand back to the front seat. The exchange did not escape Grandmother's notice, but she said nothing.

5

When we entered the house my mother said, "Maya, show your brother his room and help him hang up his clothes." She didn't have to tell me what I could do for my brother. I started for the stairs.

Grandmother said, "Sister, your mother spoke to you."

I mumbled, "Yes, ma'am."

Bailey was impressed with his room. He sat on his bed and asked, "So what is wrong? Why are you so unhappy?"

There was no reason to try to lie to him. "Well, I don't like her. I don't understand why she sent us away."

"Did you ask her?"

I said, "Of course not."

Bailey, with his usual sharpness, said, "The only thing to do is ask her."

"She's probably going to make us feel sorry for her."

"Maybe. I think she's tough. Let's go downstairs and ask her."

I held back, afraid to face her. But Bailey had never steered me wrong. He said, "Come on, My." In a second he was out the side door, so I followed.

"Mother?" He was calling her Mother already.

She stepped out of a door. "Yes?"

"My and I have a question we must ask you. You don't have to answer if you don't want to."

She said, "I know that all I really *have* to do is stay black and die. So, what is your question?"

"Why did you send us away, and why didn't you come back and get us?"

She said, "Sit down, children."

Bailey held a chair for me and we both sat down.

"Your father and I began to dislike each other almost as soon as we got married. Then both of you were born and we had to think about what we would do with you. We tried for nearly a year but we realized there was nothing that could keep us together. We fought like wild animals. His mother wrote us and said to send the children to her. When we got her letter, we went out, and for the first time in a year, we had an evening without cursing each other out and slamming out of a restaurant."

22

She started to smile. "I missed you but I knew you were in the best place for you. I would have been a terrible mother. I had no patience. Maya, when you were about two years old, you asked me for something. I was busy talking, so you hit my hand, and I slapped you off the porch without thinking. It didn't mean I didn't love you; it just meant I wasn't ready to be a mother. I'm explaining to you, not apologizing. We would have all been sorry had I kept you."

6

Soon after our arrival in California, Vivian Baxter said to me and Bailey, "Please sit down, I have something to say." Bailey looked at me and winked and we both sat on the sofa. She sat in an easy chair and said that Baxter was her maiden name and when she married our father she became a Johnson. Then they were divorced. A few years ago, she met Clidell Jackson and they loved each other, so they married. Clidell was on a business trip but would be returning soon. She said he was a wonderful man and she knew we would all get along well and love each other.

When Bailey and I were alone, we talked about our new stepfather. Bailey counseled me to not make any judgment until we saw him. I agreed.

One morning our mother walked around picking up a glass here and putting it down there, placing a plate on the table and then replacing it. Bailey said that our stepfather would be coming soon. As usual, he was right.

Mother asked us to dress nicely and to be prepared to meet our new father. We waited in the living room wondering.

We heard her open the front door and we stood.

Mother introduced us to Clidell Jackson. He was a wondrous, very pleasant-looking man, tall and large with a little paunch. His tailor-made three-piece suits made him look like a lawyer or banker. He wore a yellow diamond stickpin in his tie and his shirt had starched collars and cuffs.

When Bailey and I shook hands with him, he said, "I'm glad to meet you. I know your ages, and I know when I was fifteen, I thought I knew everything. As I grew older, I had to admit I knew either nothing or very little. I am sure you know everything, but there are a few more things I can teach you. I know every card game and betting game you've ever heard of. I want you to learn that you cannot have anything without working for it. The only way you can be taken advantage of is if you think you can get something for nothing. I'll be happy if you call me Daddy Clidell. I love your mother very much and I will always take care of the three of you."

Vivian Baxter gave us both kisses and said, "Now you can go upstairs."

On the landing outside my door, Bailey said, "I like him."

I said, "I don't know him."

He said, "Trust me, he's good. He won't try anything wrong with you and he does love our mother."

7

The time had come for Grandmother to return to Stamps. My heart beat so loudly, I thought I would burst. I had been with her so long I couldn't imagine the sun rising without my grandmother putting Vaseline on my arms and brushing my hair. But we were at the train station, Lady, Bailey, and me. We hugged Grandmother on the platform and Bailey walked her onto the train car carrying her suitcase. Through the window I watched him bend over her as the wheels began to turn slowly. I ran to the door shouting, "Bailey, the train is leaving!"

I started up the steps and my mother caught my coat sleeve. "Get off that train. Now." Bailey came to the door and easily leapt from the train steps to the platform.

He grinned. "Here I am." He turned toward the train as it was picking up speed. He waved.

"Bye, Momma! Have a good trip!" He turned to Mother for approval, and she smiled.

He took my hand. "Come on, My. We're near the house, aren't we?"

I said, "Yeah."

He said, "We'll see you at home, Mother. We're walking. See you at home."

She said, "Okay."

He did call her Mother but he was walking home with me. I was used to doing whatever Bailey wanted me to do, and I knew she had to get used to Bailey having his way.

He began to run and I followed him. I was glad that I had my brother and a woman whom I was beginning to like, and maybe even to love. Perhaps life was going to be all right after all.

Mother called us out of our rooms and we sat in the upstairs kitchen. I was to learn that whenever she had anything important to say, she would first ask us to sit down, and then say, "I have something to say." Later, when we were not in her hearing, Bailey would imitate her: "Sit down, I have something to say."

She always had something to say. She had brought soft drinks up from the downstairs refrigerator. She asked me to fill two glasses with ice and told Bailey to go downstairs and tell Papa Ford that she wanted a drink and Bailey should bring it to her.

Papa Ford was the houseman and cook who lived with us.

Without speaking to me, she filled our glasses with colas. When Bailey returned with her drink of whiskey on the rocks, she clicked our glasses and said, "Now you say, 'Skoal.'" We did so.

Then she sat. "Clidell Jackson is from Slayton, Texas. He went to the third grade in school. He can read and write, just barely, but he is considered one of the best gamblers on the West Coast. Also, he never cheats and he never allows a cheater in any of his gambling houses. He is a kind man, someone I admire and want around my children.

"Remember this: Your reputation is the most important thing you'll ever have. Not clothes, nor money, not the big cars you may drive. If your reputation is good, you can achieve anything you want in the world. I know your Grandmother Henderson told you that—maybe not in the same words I'm using, but I'm sure as you live here with me, and Daddy Clidell, you will learn that we do not lie, and we do not cheat, and we do laugh a lot. At ourselves first, and then at each other.

"Papa Ford cleans and cooks and sends clothes to the laundry and cleaners. You will clean your own rooms and you will respect him. He is a worker, not a slave."

I was liking her.

Daddy Clidell, Papa Ford, Bailey, and I were standing at the kitchen table, waiting for Mother. She came to the door and announced, "Everyone please come into the dining room." Bailey and I looked at each other, puzzled. We only sat in the dining room on Sundays or when we had guests.

"Come in, I have something to say."

Daddy Clidell sat down, and the rest of us sat at our places, which as usual were set.

Mother waved away the hands that were waiting for the ritual of blessing the table.

"No, not that," she said. "I have learned that Maya doesn't want to call me Mother. She has another name for me. It seems like I don't fit her image of a mother." Everyone looked at me disapprovingly, even Bailey. "She wants to call me 'Lady.'" She waited a second, then said, "And I like it. She said I'm beautiful and kind, so I resemble a true lady. From now on, Junior, you can call me Lady. In fact, I'm going to introduce myself to people as Lady Jackson. You all feel free to call me Lady. Everybody has the right to be called anything he wants to be called. I want to be called Lady."

Bailey jumped into her speech. "Then I want to be called Bailey. I hate Junior. I am no little boy."

There were a few seconds of quiet.

"Then that's what you'll be called. Clidell, what about you?"

"I'll go on being Daddy Clidell."

Papa Ford said, "I'll go on being called Papa Ford. Having said that, can I call you all to dinner at the kitchen table? It's ready to be called Dinner."

We all laughed, and what could have been a stiff session was made light, yet serious.

I smiled at "Lady." She handled introducing her new name to the family with grace. It was difficult to resist her.

8

I picked up the telephone and said "Hello." Lady said to me, "Hi, baby, I'm out on my own recognizance."

I didn't know what that meant but it sounded like a good thing so I said, "I'm glad." She asked to speak to my dad so I took the phone to him.

About two months later, I learned what the phrase "own recognizance" meant. She had been arrested for gambling and then released without bail.

One Sunday morning, a few weeks later, she was arrested again and had to be bailed out of jail. A woman she knew slightly had gone with her to church. After services they went to a supermarket. Mother picked up what she wanted and her friend picked up something, paid, and then they sat outside of the supermarket waiting for their car. The woman opened her jacket and showed my mother that she had stolen a two-pound can of coffee. My mother said, "You're stupid. Take it back."

The woman said, "I've stolen this. You can have half of it if you want."

My mother said, "Take it back or I will take care of you."

The woman said, "Are you kidding?"

My mother hit her and the police were called and both women were taken to jail. She didn't telephone me, but rather called Boyd Puccinelli, a bail bondsman, who was also a friend.

When she came home I said, "I'm sorry you weren't released on your own recognizance, and that you had to be bailed out."

She said, "That's nothing. I don't like to go to jail, because it takes up my time. But it doesn't frighten me; jail was made for people, not horses. I'll be damned if I want to go to jail for stealing a lousy can of coffee."

Bailey and I were woven fairly smoothly into Vivian Baxter's big-city ways. Bailey was generally more willing than I was to blend into our mother's life. For the most part he adored our mother, and laughing and joking, he showed his delight at being with her. However, on the odd occasion when he remembered the lonely nights in Arkansas, his angry personality came to the fore.

He would speak loudly and angrily and would walk out of rooms and slam doors behind himself. He never went too far, knowing that Vivian would snatch him back if he stepped over the bounds of courtesy she imposed. He did let her know sometimes that he had not forgotten being abandoned.

I was almost fourteen and had been living with my mother and my stepfather for a few months. She found that I didn't lie easily. Not because I was so righteous, but because I was simply too proud to be caught in a lie and be forced to apologize. Lady didn't lie, either, but she explained that it was in fact because she was too mean to lie.

She admired my decision to tell the truth at all costs. She gave me a key to her money closet, where she kept thousands of dollars and cases of liquor. The time was World War II and whiskey was not only rare and expensive, it was rationed. So she always kept the booze in a locked closet with the money.

One morning I was sitting at the kitchen with Mother and five or six women who worked in her gambling casinos.

Mother said to the general company, "Liquor has been escaping from my closet and only Papa Ford and

Maya have keys, other than the two that I and Daddy Clidell have."

She looked at me and said, "So, baby, have you been drinking the whiskey?" And I said, "No, I have not."

She said, "All right." Then she went on talking casually. But when I started to get up she said, "Okay, all right, darling, go on. I believe you. You said you didn't know anything about the whiskey."

I said, "Wait, I didn't say I didn't know anything about it, I said I had not been drinking it."

She said, "Oh, sit down." So I sat down. She said, "So what about it?"

I said, "I have been taking some of it to the New Fillmore Theater movie house on Sundays."

She said, "What do you mean?"

I said, "I pour some of the liquor into a mason jar and take it to the movie house on Sundays."

"What do you do with it?"

I said, "I give it to the kids. I want them to like me."

"You've been taking my liquor out of my house and taking it to the movie house and giving it to underage children? Do you realize how stupid that is? Do you realize how much money that costs me and do you realize I can go to jail for all that?"

She was embarrassing me in front of the women.

I said, "Please, Lady, don't make such a big thing out of it. There are only sixteen shots in a bottle and they only cost a dollar twenty-five a shot."

She reached across the table and tried to slap me but her arm was too short. Had she succeeded it would have been one of three times in my life that she hit me. I stood up. I couldn't believe that she would slap me in front of those women.

"You, do you realize how stupid that is?"

I mumbled and walked upstairs to my room. I sat on the bed and thought, What am I to do now? I was wrong. I had stolen her whiskey and had been embarrassed in front of people only a little older than I. I waited for my mother to come upstairs but she didn't come.

When Bailey came home, I called him into my room and told him what I had said and what I had done. Bailey, my boon, my brother, my heart, my Kingdom Come, said, "You are stupid." That brought me to tears. He said, "Do you realize it's against the law, and it's costing our mother all this money, and she can go to jail for you bringing liquor to underage kids? That is really stupid." He walked out.

So this time I really cried. When I calmed down, I decided it was my time to apologize to Vivian Baxter.

I collected myself and waited to hear when all the other people had gone. I knocked at her bedroom door. She said, "Come in."

I went in and said, "I want to speak to you." She was as cold as an iceberg.

She said, "Yes?"

I said, "I was wrong and I beg your pardon, and I will never do anything like that again. I didn't think first, and I beg your pardon." She softened as an ice cube would in a pan over a blazing fire.

She said, "I accept your apology."

She embraced me, and I don't think we ever mentioned the matter again. I had almost forgotten it, but I wanted to share it here because there are times when no one is right, and sometimes among family and children, no one can admit that there is no right, and that maybe at the same time there is no wrong. But in this case I was wrong and I appreciate Vivian Baxter for being big enough to accept my apology.

9

Neither my brother nor I had any idea of what our father was like, but Mother thought that at least he should get to know his children. She arranged for us to visit him separately in San Diego. Bailey Jr. was the first to go. He went down the second summer after we returned to California. When he came back, he made a nice face when Mother asked how much he had enjoyed the visit.

He said, "The house was clean and Daddy Bailey cooks well. He and his wife like classical music. They play Bach and Beethoven loudly on their very big music machine."

When we were alone he said to me, "Well, I've done that. I don't have to do it again."

I had to be next to visit my father for three weeks. He had lied to his young wife about me and about my age. He had lied about Bailey's age as well, but at

least Bailey was short and so charming that he capti-
vated her.

She and I had arranged that we would recognize
each other by the red carnations we would wear. Loretta met me at the train station.

I saw her first and when I did, I wanted to shrink
and I wished I hadn't come. She was small like
Mother but half her age. She wore a brown and
white seersucker suit with brown and white specta-
tor pumps. She carried a matching purse. She saw
me and looked twice at my carnation. Her face registered utter disbelief. I walked over to her so she
had to admit that her eyes were not playing tricks. I
was indeed Bailey Johnson's daughter and by asso-
ciation, despite my size and plainness, I was hers as
well.

I said, "Hello, Mrs. Johnson. I am Maya, your
husband's daughter. Bailey Johnson is my father.
What shall I call you?" I was twice her size and my
voice sounded adult.

His name brought her out of the shock, which
had her mostly immobilized. I could hear the locks
slam shut in her mind. She would never accept me as
anyone close to her.

My stepmother drove me to a pretty little bunga-
low. She did not initiate any conversation during the

ride. She answered each question I asked with a single yes or no.

Inside the house, Bailey Sr. filled the small living room. His wife sat on the sofa, still wrapped in silence.

My father said to me, "So you're Marguerite. You look like my mother. You got here all right? Look at you; you're nearly tall as I am." His wife looked up at him but didn't speak. I was not being complimented. His statement about my height made me think he wanted me to apologize for it.

During the next three summer weeks in National City, California, relations did not improve in the Bailey Johnson Sr. household.

My father and Loretta left for work at the same time each morning. They had little to say to me. I found the nearest library and since I had recently discovered Thomas Wolfe, I read *You Can't Go Home Again* and *Look Homeward, Angel*.

I was careful with the money Mother had given me for vacation. The San Diego Zoo was cheap, and the movie matinee prices were just fine.

I learned very little about my stepmother. She had graduated from Prairie View A&M University, a highly respected black university. Its graduates are known to be extremely proud of its history. My father was a dietitian at the naval base. He brought home large packages of thinly sliced ham and turkey and bologna. The meats looked like those bought in the supermarket but they weren't wrapped in supermarket paper. I hated to think my father was stealing food from his job, but it seemed so.

I telephoned my mother twice and told her all was well. She didn't know my telephone voice well enough to question what I said.

The long, hot, hateful San Diego summer was almost over. I was eager to leave my father's stiff, unfriendly house. I wanted to be back home with my mother and her rooms filled with laughter and loud jazz.

On my last week in Southern California, my father announced that he was going to take me to Mexico. Loretta and I were in agreement: She didn't want him to take me and I did not want to go.

My father drove us to a small village about thirty miles beyond Tijuana. We stopped at a cantina. I knew he spoke Spanish, but I was surprised that he was so fluent. After studying Spanish for two years, I was a little jealous that he spoke so much better than I. He went into the cantina, leaving me in the car. I decided to go into the cantina and ask him to take me home, but before I could move, he came back with a woman who had two tots, who looked like me and my brother. They smiled and greeted me in Spanish. My father picked up the children and cuddled them.

He asked me to join him and the Mexican family in the cantina. He sat in a booth and talked to the woman and drank until he was sloppy drunk. It was getting dark and I was becoming very uncomfortable.

The mother of the children had sent them away and I asked her to help me put my father in the car. I opened the back door and we pushed him into the backseat. He stumbled in and fell asleep immediately.

I got into the driver's seat and thanked the woman. I had never even taken a driving lesson but I had watched people work the manual transmissions. I put my foot on the clutch and shifted gears, and the car jumped and bumped and carried on. I learned that I shouldn't take my foot off the clutch right away, but rather ease it off. I drove.

Sometimes the car would almost stall and I would wait, then quickly put my foot on the clutch and slowly put the other foot on the gas and raise the clutch easily, easily. The road wound around a mountain. I didn't know what I would do if another car came toward me. But not one did and I finally got down off the mountain and back to the border.

One of the border guards, who had seen me and

my father pass through before, came over whistling and flirting. He looked in and asked me in Spanish, "He's drunk, huh?" I didn't know the word for drunk but I could tell from the way he grinned that he knew.

I said, "Sí, como always."

I drove from the border straight to my father's house and got out of the car. His wife was angry.

My father woke up enough to lurch into the house, right past her and on into the bedroom.

She directed her anger at him my way. "You have made your father drunk. You are so stupid. You are both so stupid."

Then she added, "You are such a nasty thing."

She was rude, I said, and, "Well, I'll be going back to my mother tomorrow."

She flared up further: "You can go to her right now. She's a whore."

I lunged at her. "You can't call my mother that!" She had her sewing scissors in her hand and cut me.

She gave me a towel to put around my waist, and then woke up my father. Hungover, stinking and fumbling, he took me to a friend's house, where they put Band-Aids over the cut.

My father left me there and after a little stiff conversation his friend went to sleep. I stayed awake all night. The next morning my father came to see about me. His friend had gone to work. All he said was "Don't worry about a thing. I won't let Loretta cut you again." He was smiling as if the incident were negligible, and I also didn't like the way he hugged me and said, "You don't have to go home. I will take care of you." He left but I found no comfort in his words. I knew he didn't want to take care of me the way I needed to be taken care of.

I made myself a big sandwich and left. I still had the keys to my father's house. I knew he and his wife were at work. I went into the house and gathered a few clothes and put them into an overnight suitcase. I wasn't careful in selecting the clothes because I wanted to be out of their house as quickly as possible.

I left their keys on the hall table and slammed the door after myself. I went to the bus terminal and put my bag into a locker, then went walking into the sunlit streets of San Diego. I was excited and totally unafraid, which proved that I was too young to understand the predicament I was in.

I walked the streets until I found an old junkyard. After prowling through it I found a neat and clean wreck that I thought would be a good place to sleep. I had a little of the money left that Mother had given me and I went to a matinee.

When it began to get dark, I went back to the

junkyard. This time I discovered a nicer and cleaner car. No sooner had I fallen asleep in it than noise awakened me. I sat up and looked out the windows; about fifteen kids circled the car. They asked, "Who are you? Where are you going? What are you doing, and why are you here?"

I rolled down the windows and told them that I had no home and I was going to sleep in the car.

They said, "We all sleep here." There were white kids, black kids, and Spanish-speaking kids. For varying reasons, they had no place to sleep, either. They allowed me to join them.

I made a friend of a girl named Bea, my first white friend. She was just like me, only at seventeen a little older and a lot wiser. The kids all worked together. Girls had to find Coca-Cola, 7-Up, and RC Cola bottles to turn in for the deposit. The fellows worked at mowing lawns and running errands for people. There was a bakery where a black janitor gave us tote bags full of broken cookies and stale rolls. We bought milk from the supermarket. Then we would all eat and enjoy ourselves. I thought it was a wonderful way to live. I retrieved my bag from the bus station locker and washed my clothes in a Laundromat along with the other girls. I wanted to stay there until my wound had healed, because if my mother saw that I had been cut, she would make someone pay.

When I was healed I called her and said I was ready to come home. I told her if she would send a ticket to the train station, I would pick it up and take the train home. She did so and I headed back to San Francisco, putting an end to that awful and peculiar summer.

10

When I finally arrived in San Francisco, my mother said, "You know you are late for school, but you are already a semester and a half ahead of yourself. If you don't want to go to school this semester, you don't have to, but you have to get a job."

I said, "I'll get a job."

"What do you want to do?"

I said, "I want to be a conductorette on a streetcar." I had seen women on the streetcars with their little moneychanging belts and with bibs on their caps and well-fitted uniforms. I hadn't considered that all the women were white. I simply told my mother I wanted to become a conductorette.

She said, "Then go down and apply for the job."

I went to the company office, but no one would even give me an application. Back home, I told Mother. She asked me, "Why not? Do you know why they wouldn't?"

I said, "Yes, it is because I am a Negro."

She asked me, "But do you still want the job?"

I said, "Yes."

She said, "*Go get it*. You know how to order good food in a restaurant. I will give you money for that. You go to the office before the secretaries arrive. When they enter, you go in and sit down. Take one of your big thick Russian books." I was reading Tolstoy and Dostoevsky.

"Now when they go to lunch, you go to lunch, but you let them leave first. You give yourself a good quick lunch, go back, and be there before the secretaries return."

I did just that.

That was among the most hateful, awful, awkward experiences I can remember. I knew some of the girls from George Washington High School, and I had helped a few of them with their homework. They graduated and got jobs in the office where I was sitting. They would pass me laughing, making faces and pooching out their lips, laughing at my features and my hair. They whispered terrible words, racial pejoratives.

The third day I wanted to stay home, but I couldn't face Vivian Baxter. I couldn't tell her I wasn't as strong as she thought I was.

I stuck it out for two weeks until a man I had not

seen before invited me to come into his office. He asked, "Why do you want a job with the railway company?"

I said, "Because I like the uniforms, and I like people."

He said, "What experience do you have?"

I had to lie, "I was a chaufferette for Mrs. Annie Henderson in Stamps, Arkansas." My grandmother had hardly ever been in a car, let alone had a chauffeur to drive it for her.

But I got the job, and the newspapers wrote, "Maya Johnson is the first American Negro to work on the railway."

Unfortunately, a man later went down to the newspaper office and said that I was not the first black person to work there, that he had been working there for twenty years. He had been passing for white. He was fired. The company explained it was because he had lied on his initial application.

I got the job and a punishing split shift. I was to work from 4 A.M. to 8 A.M. and then 1 P.M. to 5 P.M. I knew the streetcar barn was out near the beach and I had to find a way to get there by 4 A.M.

My mother said, "Don't worry about it. I'll take you."

The first day, when my uniform arrived and it fit me well, I felt like a woman. My mother, who had run a bath for me, awakened me and complimented me on my uniform. We got into her car and she drove to the beach. When I thanked her and said, "Go home and take care of yourself," she said, "I mean to take care of the both of us." For the first time I saw the pistol on the seat. She said she would follow the car until first light, when she would honk her horn and blow me a kiss, turn away, and drive home.

For the months that I worked on the streetcar, my mother's routine never changed. I left the job when it was time to return to school.

My mother asked me to have a cup of coffee with her in the kitchen.

She said, "So, you got the job and I also got the job. You were conductorette and I was your security every day until dawn. What did you learn from this experience?"

I said, "I learned that you were probably the best protection I will ever have."

She asked, "What did you learn about yourself?"

I said, "I learned I am not afraid to work, and that's about all."

She said, "No, you learned that you have power—power and determination. I love you and I am proud of you. With those two things, you can go anywhere and everywhere."

11

At fifteen, I was allowed to stay out until eleven at night only if Bailey was along. Mother knew he would not only tell me what to do, he would tell others what they could and could not do, with me and around me.

The teenagers in the Booker T. Washington Center were restless. One night the directors refused to allow us to have a dance because one had been held the night before and we were allowed only one dance per week.

A shout lifted above our heads. "Let's go to the Mission District and eat tamales!"

Another person yelled, "Let's go to the Mission District and liberate a few dozen tacos and tamales!" There was a loud roar of agreement and I was swept along. We were on the outskirts of the Fillmore District before I realized Bailey was missing. He had not come with me to the center that evening.

I knew what I should do, but I could not bring myself to say that I had to leave and go home. We rode streetcars to the largely Mexican area. The aroma wafting from the cantinas and the music of the mariachi bands were calling for us. We danced in the streets. Boys and girls flirted and then ordered more tamales and tacos. We all spoke a little Spanish but we acted as if we spoke more. Someone announced it was one o'clock.

The enormity of my lateness made me dumb. When I found my voice, I said, "I've got to get home."

Alarmed voices joined mine.

"God, how did it get so late?"

"I'm going to get killed."

"God, what kind of lie can I work up this time?"

We counted our money, but we didn't have enough for carfare for everyone to get home safely. Along with two other girls and one boy, I walked home from the Mission District to the Fillmore District.

It was a long trek, and although we started it with trepidation, we began to brighten as we neared home. We did begin to see the absurdity of our situation. We were going to get in trouble over some tacos and tamales, which we didn't need, and that made us laugh. Tamales and tacos had made us break the rules.

I parted with my friends and walked the last block to my house as fast as I could. I was still in a pleasant mood so I ran up the two marble steps to the French doors. When I put my key into the lock and pushed the door, it was pushed back at me with enormous force.

My mother stepped out onto the landing. She held a ring of keys in her fist. She said, "Goddamnit!" and hit me in the face.

As I screamed, she grabbed my coat and pulled me into the house. She was cursing and shouting at me and at the walls and at the windows.

"Where in the hell have you been? Even whores are in bed. My fifteen-year-old daughter is roaming the streets."

I tasted blood as it slipped into my mouth. Mother continued to rant and I heard doors open and voices.

"Lady, are you all right?"

My stepfather: "What's going on? I'm on my way."

Papa Ford came shuffling down the hall in his cotton robe. "What's happening? What's going on, Vivian?"

In the critical moment, he stopped being the houseman, the cook, the servant, and became her father, or doting uncle. He asked me, "Where the hell have you been?"

I was crying too hard to answer.

Suddenly Bailey appeared, also in his robe, also in control of himself. He saw my face and heard Mother's tirade. He said with authority, "Come on, Maya. Come upstairs. I'll get some towels. Go to your room."

I followed him up the stairs and went to my room. I was sitting on the bed when he came in bringing a warm, wet soapy towel in one hand and a dry, fluffy towel in the other. He said, "Don't try to talk. Just calm down and clean your face. I'm going back to my room. Don't worry about anything. I'll figure out what we're going to do."

I cleaned up and managed to relax because my big brother was in charge. I did not catch the irony that at fifteen, I was six feet tall and Bailey at seventeen was five foot five.

The next morning the image in the bathroom mirror shocked me. My eyes were black and my lips were swollen. I had begun crying again when Bailey appeared with the suitcase.

He said, "You look awful. I'm so sorry, Maya. Come on." He guided me back from the bathroom to my bedroom.

"Pack two sets of underclothes, two skirts, and two sweaters. We're leaving this place."

I found some clothes, folded them, and put them in the suitcase, which he closed.

"Where are we going?"

"I don't know yet, but anywhere away from here."

I followed him down the steps. At the bottom, my mother stood with her arms akimbo.

"Where the hell do you think you're going?"

Before Bailey could answer, she looked up the steps and saw me. She screamed and reeled as if she was going to fall.

She said, "My baby, oh, my baby! Come here! I'm so sorry!"

Bailey stared straight at her. "We are leaving your house. Nobody, but nobody, beats up my baby sister." Bailey took my hand.

Mother said, "Baby, I'm so sorry, so sorry."

Bailey said, "Maya, let's go!"

My mother turned to Bailey and said, "Please give me a chance. Please. Come in the kitchen and give me a chance."

We followed her to the kitchen, where my stepfather and Papa Ford were drinking coffee. Each looked at me, and the shock on their faces was undeniable.

My mother asked, "Would you please go into the

dining room or the living room? I have to talk to my children."

The three of us were left in the warm, aromatic air of the kitchen. My mother took a tea cloth off a rack and put it on the floor. She asked me and Bailey to sit on the kitchen chairs. Vivian Baxter got down on her knees and prayed to God to ask forgiveness, and then in the same quivering voice, she begged me to forgive her.

"I was crazy. I was out of my mind. I remembered what that bastard had done to you when you were seven years old. I couldn't imagine someone else taking you, abusing you, and maybe even killing you. I had just left your empty room when I came down the stairs and suddenly you were at the door, opening it with a smile on your face. I had the key ring in my hand with at least twenty keys on it and I hit you without thinking."

She turned to Bailey. "I didn't mean to hurt your sister. I beg you to forgive me." Then she began to cry so piteously that Bailey and I left our chairs and joined her on the floor, where we cradled her in our arms.

Mother resisted our attempts to encourage her to stand up, so we went upstairs to our rooms. Bailey said, "She's a strong woman, a very strong woman."

"I wish she had knelt down and apologized in front of Daddy Clidell and Papa Ford."

"No, she couldn't do that. It would have taken away some of the power she has over them."

"Well, we took away the power she had over us."

"No, we didn't take it, honey, she gave it to us."

12

Bailey knocked on my door. I saw his face and knew that Armageddon had arrived. "What is it?" I asked.

He pushed me aside and entered my room. "I'm leaving. I'm going to join the army or navy." He had been crying. "I'm of age: I'm seventeen."

"Why? You're supposed to graduate next month! Why?"

"I'm not going to wait that long."

"Is it something Lady did?"

He said, "I should have gone back with Grandmother. She needs me."

I said, "Lady needs you. She adores you. You ought to see the way she looks at you."

"She's got Daddy Clidell, and Papa Ford, and you, and . . . and . . . you know that guy named Buddy?"

Buddy was a frequent visitor, often taking over the conversation, telling jokes and making fun of the local politicians. Lady and Daddy Clidell both were amused by Buddy.

"What about Buddy . . . What?"

Bailey asked, "Did you ever see how she looked at him?"

"No," I said.

"Well, I did, and I'd be surprised if they weren't off doing it in some motel."

I said, "Bailey, you ought to be ashamed. Do you think our mother is committing adultery?"

"I wouldn't put it past her. She gave us away, right? She abandoned her own children. Why wouldn't she commit adultery?"

"Bailey, tell me straight: Did you see anything that could make you sure?"

"No, not really, except the way she looks at him."

"Well, I don't believe it. I'm just starting to really like her and I don't think she would betray Daddy Clidell."

He opened my door and turned to look at me, almost sneering.

"You'd have to be a man to understand that, and you're just a girl." He went out and slammed my door.

I didn't know what to do. Obviously I could not tattle on my brother. All I could do was try to talk him out of his decision to join the service. I went to his room but he wouldn't answer the door. He avoided me for about a month. Then one evening at the dinner table he said, "I have an announcement to make!"

He put some papers on the table.

"I've joined the merchant marine. I've passed the exams and the physical tests. I'll ship out soon."

Mother reached for the papers but he snatched them back.

She said, "You can't. I won't let you."

"I've done it already. I am of age. It's too late anyway. I've already sworn in."

Mother fell back in her chair. "Why? You're supposed to graduate in a few weeks. I've just bought new clothes I was going to wear."

Bailey said, "As usual, you think it's only about you."

Mother said, "But why? Why? Maya, did you know?"

Bailey looked at me and said, "My didn't know about this. It's only for me to know and you to wonder, or maybe you can mention me to Buddy."

Vivian was surprised. "You're angry with me? Why? What have I done to you? What does Buddy have to do with you joining the service?"

Bailey looked at Mother scornfully. I felt sorry for her, and for him.

Weeks later Bailey was gone. Mother and I both missed him badly, but it was too painful to talk about his absence, and so we never mentioned it.

She began to pack bags for a couple of months' journey. She had to go back to Alaska to see about the gambling joints she and Daddy Clidell owned in Nome.

13

I was distressed because I didn't develop like other girls. I didn't have breasts, really plump breasts. I had little nubs on my chest, but nothing substantial. My buttocks were flat; my legs were too thin and too long. My voice was deep. To add to my woes, I thought that I might grow up to be a lesbian. I had read a book called *The Well,* purportedly written by a lesbian. She was grossly unhappy, and her friends who were also lesbians were miserable as well. My slow physical developments made me wonder if just possibly I would grow up to become a lesbian and be unhappy. I certainly didn't want that.

Still, not all the boys were after only pretty girls. Some let me know that they would like to make love to me, or at least have sex with me. They were only teenagers, and it was easy to ignore them. But there was Babe, who lived up the block from me. He was nineteen years old and very handsome. I developed a dizzying infatuation for him. For weeks I imagined how it would be to rest in his arms. His usual approach to me was "Hey Maya, when you gonna give me some of that long, tall goodie?"

One day as I was passing by him, I stopped spontaneously and before he could speak I said, "Hi, Babe. Do you still want some of this long, tall goodie?" He almost dropped the toothpick out of his mouth.

But he quickly recovered. "Yes, let's go." He had a friend who had a room he could use. He didn't ask why I was willing to go with him. In fact, we were silent as we walked the few blocks to a large, typical San Francisco house. He used a key and opened the door. In the bedroom there was no kissing or foreplay. No coddling and whispering; none of that. Just "get your pants down" and then sex.

I had been raped when I was seven and I had seen the rapist's privates. My brother was too careful to let me see him naked so I really had never seen any man nude except the rapist. That evening I caught a glimpse of Babe's privates and it embarrassed me. I was sorry I had been so bold.

I knew I was going to tell Bailey eventually—and I knew he was going to tell me I had again done something stupid.

Babe made a loud sound and then lay still. That's when I knew we had finished having sex. He started to get up and I asked him, "Is this all it is?"

He said, "Yeah."

I dressed, really disappointed that having sex had not assured me that I was normal and not a lesbian. We left the house. I wanted to discuss the incident with my brother, but he was in the merchant marine and was not due to return to San Francisco for months.

Two months passed and I found that I was pregnant. I called Babe and invited him over to my house. When I told him that I was pregnant, he acted as if he were about four years old. He whined, "I'm not the father. Don't tell that lie. Don't lie on me."

So I said, "You may leave." I could be very high-handed when I was young. "You may go out. Go out the back door."

When my mother returned to San Francisco and then went back to Alaska, I did not tell her about my pregnancy. I was afraid she would take me out of school. But when Bailey came home on merchant marine leave, I told him I was pregnant. He warned me, "Don't tell Mother. She'll take you out of school.

You must finish high school now. If you don't, you might never go back. You get that diploma."

Mother made repeated trips to Alaska to tend to their affairs, so she missed watching me blossom into a soon-to-be mother.

My stepfather was around and noticed a difference but didn't know what he was seeing. He said, "You're growing up, beginning to look like a young woman."

I thought, I should: I'm over eight months pregnant.

And Papa Ford, who cleaned the house and cooked, didn't notice me at all.

I went to school unsteadily all summer—sometimes nausea forced me off the streetcars—but I finished my senior year at Mission High's summer school.

Daddy Clidell's birthday and V-Day coincided with my graduation. My dad took me out to a congratulatory dinner and told me how proud he was to have a daughter who had graduated from high school. He reminded me that he had gotten only to third grade. We came back home and I went upstairs to my room and wrote a letter.

"Dear Dad, I am sorry I have brought disrespect and scandal on the family, but I am pregnant." I put the page on his pillow.

It was impossible to find sleep. I waited to hear his footsteps. What would he do? He might curse me out. No, he never cursed. At about four o'clock in the morning he came home. I thought surely he would read that note and come stomping up the steps. Nothing. I took a bath, then I gave up trying to sleep and sat on the side of the bed. At nine o'clock that morning, he called from downstairs.

"Maya, come on down. Come down and have coffee with me. I got your letter." I was dressed and nervous. He was sitting at the kitchen table and said, in his regular voice, "Now baby, I got your note. Now, um, how far are you gone?"

I caught my breath, then told him I had about three weeks before the baby would be born.

"All right, I'll call your mother. She will take care of this, don't worry. Now, I don't think you are sup-posed to do much jumping around in your condition. I see you did not get much sleep. Go back to bed."

Surprised and relieved, I went back to my room.

The next day my mother flew in from Nome. I had no idea what she was going to do. I thought of how she would look at me. I was six feet tall and very pregnant, as well as guilty and scared. She was about five feet, four and a half inches tall and very beautiful. She came in and looked at me and she said, "Oh, you're more than any three weeks pregnant."

I said, "Yes, ma'am, it is three weeks before I have the baby."

She said Daddy Clidell had misunderstood and told her on the phone that I was three weeks pregnant and she'd better come home. I looked at her and could not think of a word to say.

"All right now, baby, go run me a bath." In our family, for some unknown reason, we consider it an honor to run a bath, to put in bubbles and good scents for another person.

So I ran the bath, then, after she got in, she called to me and said, "Come and sit in here with me."

I sat on a stool in the bathroom.

"Do you smoke?"

"Yes, ma'am, but I don't have any."

She said, "Well, what do you smoke?"

"Pall Malls."

She said, "All right. I smoke Lucky Strikes, but you can have one of mine." So I had a cigarette and then she asked me, "Do you know who the father is?"

"Yes, ma'am, it was only one time."

"Do you love him?"

I said, "No."

"Does he love you?"

I said, "No."

"Well then, that's that. We will not ruin three

lives. We—*you and I*—and this family are going to have a wonderful baby. That's all there is to that. Thank you, baby. Go on."

I left the bathroom, tears of relief bathing my face. She didn't hate me or cause me to hate myself. She gave me the same respect she had always shown. She cared for me and for my child. She talked to me.

Mother stayed in the house for the three weeks, talking to me, telling family stories about babies and pregnancies and delivering babies. She recounted the night I was born. She described how long she had been in labor and how she stuffed her mouth with towels so no one would hear her cries.

When the contractions began, I got my hospital suitcase, which she had packed, and knocked on her door. When I announced I was ready to go she laughed and said, "Not yet, baby, you have a few hours. They will come slowly at first and they will get faster. Don't worry. I promise to get you to the hospital on time."

She invited me into her bedroom and gave me a bath. She put me on her bed and she shaved me in preparation for delivery.

Vivian Baxter was, among other things, a registered nurse. In the three weeks she had been home, she had taken me twice to see Dr. Rubinstein, her doctor. He had calculated the delivery date. My mother called him, left a message, and took me to the hospital.

When we arrived we could see two nurses through the glass in the door. My mother said, "Now this large one is going to be very jovial and the little one is going to be sour as a lemon. I'll bet you fifty cents."

The two women opened the door and the fat woman said, "Oh welcome! We're waiting for her. Bring her in here."

The little one said with a sour voice, "We thought you'd be here sooner." It was just as if my mother had known them before.

She told them she was a nurse, and told them the hospital where she had worked. She took me into the delivery room. The contractions came faster but the doctor didn't arrive.

Mother called one of the nurses and said that I was already shaved, and then she washed me again. My mother got up on the delivery table with me and knelt. She put one of my legs against her shoulder and took both my hands. Then she told me filthy stories, jokes. She timed the punch lines with the contractions and I would laugh. She encouraged me: "That's right, bear down, bear down." I bore down and as the baby was coming out she said, "Here he comes, and he has black hair."

I wondered, What color hair did you think he would have?

The nurse washed him and my mother said, "Look at this: We have a wonderful handsome boy. Okay baby, it's all right now. You can go to sleep."

She kissed me and left. My stepdad later told me she was so wrung out when she got home, she looked like she had had twins.

I thought about my mother and knew she was amazing. She never made me feel as if I brought scandal to the family. The baby had not been planned and I would have to rethink plans about education, but to Vivian Baxter that was life being life. Having a baby while I was unmarried had not been wrong. It was simply slightly inconvenient.

I found a job when my son was two months old. I went to Mother and told her, "Mother, I am going to move."

"You are going to leave my house?" She was shocked that I would leave her fine home, with all its amenities.

I said, "Yes, I have found a job, and a room with cooking privileges down the hall, and the landlady will be the babysitter."

She looked at me half pityingly and half proud. She said, "All right, you go, but remember this: When you cross my doorstep, you have already been raised.

With what you have learned from your Grandmother Henderson in Arkansas and what you have learned from me, you know the difference between right and wrong. Do right. Don't let anybody raise you from the way you have been raised. Know you will always have to make adaptations, in love relationships, in friends, in society, in work, but don't let anybody change your mind. And then remember this: You can always come home."

I walked away and was back in my bedroom before I heard my own words echoing in my mind. I had called Lady "Mother." I knew she had noticed but we never ever mentioned the incident. I was aware that after the birth of my son and the decision to move and get a place for just the two of us, I thought of Vivian Baxter as my mother. On the odd occasion and out of habit, sometimes I called her Lady, but her treatment of me and her love for my baby earned her the right to be called Mother. On the day we moved from her house, Mother liberated me by letting me know she was on my side. I realized that I had grown close to her and that she had liberated me. She liberated me from a society that would have had me think of myself as the lower of the low. She liberated me to life. And from that time to this time, I have taken life by the lapels and I have said, "I'm with you, kid."

71

ME
& MOM

*"I will look after you and I will look after anybody you say
needs to be looked after, any way you say. I am here.
I brought my whole self to you. I am your mother."*

(1986)

14

Independence is a heady draft, and if you drink it in your youth, it can have the same effect on the brain as young wine does. It does not matter that its taste is not always appealing. It is addictive and with each drink you want more.

By the time I was twenty-two I was living in San Francisco. I had a five-year-old son, two jobs, and two rented rooms, with cooking privileges down the hall. My landlady, Mrs. Jefferson, was kind and grand-motherly. She was a ready babysitter and insisted on providing dinner for her tenants. Her ways were so tender and her personality so sweet that no one was mean enough to discourage her disastrous culinary exploits. Spaghetti at her table, which was offered at least three times a week, was a mysterious red, white, and brown concoction. We would occasionally en-counter an unidentifiable piece of meat hidden among the pasta.

There was no money in my budget for restaurant food, so I and my son, Guy, were always loyal, if often unhappy, diners at Chez Jefferson.

My mother had moved into another large Victorian house, on Fulton Street, which she again filled with Gothic, heavily carved furniture. The upholstery on the sofa and occasional chairs was red-wine-colored mohair. Oriental rugs were placed throughout the house. She had a live-in employee, Poppa, who cleaned the house and sometimes filled in as cook helper.

Mother picked up Guy twice a week and took him to her house, where she fed him peaches and cream and hot dogs, but I only went to Fulton Street once a month and at an agreed-upon time.

She understood and encouraged my self-reliance and I looked forward eagerly to our standing appointment. On the occasion, she would cook one of my favorite dishes. One lunch date stands out in my mind. I call it Vivian's Red Rice Day.

When I arrived at the Fulton Street house my mother was dressed beautifully. Her makeup was perfect and she wore good jewelry.

After we embraced, I washed my hands and we walked through her formal, dark dining room and into the large, bright kitchen.

Much of lunch was already on the kitchen table.

Vivian Baxter was very serious about her delicious meals.

On that long-ago Red Rice Day, my mother had offered me a crispy, dry-roasted capon, no dressing or gravy, and a simple lettuce salad, no tomatoes or cucumbers. A wide-mouthed bowl covered with a platter sat next to her plate.

She fervently blessed the food with a brief prayer and put her left hand on the platter and her right on the bowl. She turned the dishes over and gently loosened the bowl from its contents and revealed a tall mound of glistening red rice (my favorite food in the entire world) decorated with finely minced parsley and green stalks of scallions.

The chicken and salad do not feature so prominently in my taste buds' memory, but each grain of red rice is emblazoned on the surface of my tongue forever.

Gluttonous and *greedy* negatively describe the hearty eater offered the seduction of her favorite food.

Two large portions of rice sated my appetite, but the deliciousness of the dish made me long for a larger stomach so that I could eat two more helpings.

My mother had plans for the rest of her afternoon, so she gathered her wraps and we left the house together.

We reached the middle of the block and were enveloped in the stinging acid aroma of vinegar from the pickle factory on the corner of Fillmore and Fulton streets. I had walked ahead. My mother stopped me and said, "Baby."

I walked back to her.

"Baby, I've been thinking and now I am sure. You are the greatest woman I've ever met."

I looked down at the pretty little woman, with her perfect makeup and diamond earrings, and a silver fox scarf. She was admired by most people in San Francisco's black community and even some whites liked and respected her.

She continued. "You are very kind and very intelligent and those elements are not always found together. Mrs. Eleanor Roosevelt, Dr. Mary McLeod Bethune, and my mother—yes, you belong in that category. Here, give me a kiss."

She kissed me on the lips and turned and jaywalked across the street to her beige and brown Pontiac. I pulled myself together and walked down to Fillmore Street. I crossed there and waited for the number 22 streetcar.

My policy of independence would not allow me to accept money or even a ride from my mother, but I welcomed her and her wisdom. Now I thought of what she had said. I thought, Suppose she is right?

She's very intelligent and often said she didn't fear anyone enough to lie. Suppose I really am going to become somebody. Imagine.

At that moment, when I could still taste the red rice, I decided the time had come to stop my dangerous habits like smoking, drinking, and cursing. I did stop cursing but some years would pass before I came to grips with drinking and smoking.

Imagine I might really become somebody. Someday.

"Mother picked up Guy twice a week and took him to her house, where she fed him peaches and cream and hot dogs."

(Vivian Baxter, Guy Johnson, and Maya Angelou)

15

It is a story indelibly seared into my mind, and I've told part of it before.

His name was Mark. He was tall, black, and well built. If good looks were horses, he could seat the entire Royal Canadian Mounties. He wanted to become a boxer and was inspired by Joe Louis. He left his native Texas and found work in Detroit. There he intended to make enough money to find a trainer who would help him become a professional boxer.

A machine in the automotive plant cut three fingers off his right hand and his dream died when they severed. I met him in San Francisco, where he had moved, and he told me the story explaining why he was known as Two Fingers Mark. He did not show any rancor about the death of his dreams. He spoke softly and often paid for a babysitter so I could visit him in his rented room. He was an ideal suitor, a

lover with a slow hand. I felt absolutely safe and secure.

After a few months of his tender attention, he
picked me up one night from my job and said he was
taking me out to Half Moon Bay.

He parked on a cliff, and through the windows I
saw the moonlight silver on the rippling water.

I got out of the car, and when he said, "Come
over here," I went immediately.

He said, "You've got another man, and you've
been lying to me." I started to laugh. I was still laughing when he hit me. Before I could breathe he hit me
in the face with both fists. I did see stars before I fell.

When I came to, he had removed most of my
clothes and leaned me against an outcropping of rock.
He had a large wooden slat in his hand and he was
crying.

"I treated you so well, you lousy cheating, low-
down bitch." I tried to walk to him but my legs
would not support me. He turned me around. Then
he hit the back of my head with the board. I passed
out, but when I came to, I saw that he continued to
cry. He continued to beat me and I continued to pass
out.

I must depend on hearsay for the events of the
next few hours.

Mark put me into the backseat of his car and

drove to the African American area in San Francisco. He parked in front of Betty Lou's Chicken Shack and called some hangers-around and showed me to them.

"This is what you do with a lying, cheating broad."

They recognized me and returned to the restaurant. They told Miss Betty Lou that Mark had Vivian's daughter in the backseat of his car and she looked dead.

Miss Betty Lou and my mother were close friends. Miss Betty Lou phoned my mother.

No one knew where he lived or worked or even his last name.

Because of the pool halls and gambling clubs my mother owned, and the police contacts Betty Lou had, they expected to find Mark quickly.

My mother was close with the leading bail bondsman in San Francisco. So she telephoned him. Boyd Puccinelli had no Mark or Two Fingers Mark in his files.

He promised Vivian he would continue to search.

I awakened to find I was in a bed and I was sore all over. It hurt to breathe, to try to speak. Mark said that was because I had broken ribs. My lips had been speared by my teeth.

He started to cry, saying he loved me. He brought a double-edged razor blade and put it to his throat.

"I'm not worth living. I should kill myself."

I had no voice to discourage him. He quickly put the razor blade on my throat.

"I can't leave you here for some other Negro to have you." Speaking was impossible and breathing was painful.

Suddenly he changed his mind.

"You haven't eaten for three days. I've got to get you some juice. Do you like pineapple juice or orange juice? Just nod your head."

I didn't know what to do. What would send him off?

"I'm going to the corner store to get you some juice. I'm sorry I hurt you. When I come back, I'm going to nurse you back to health, full health, I promise."

I watched him leave.

Only then did I recognize that I was in his room, where I had been often. I knew his landlady lived on the same floor, and I thought that if I could get her attention, she would help me. I inhaled as much air as I could take and tried to shout, but no sounds would come. The pain of trying to sit up was so extreme that I tried only once.

I knew where he had put the razor blade. If I could get it, at least I could take my own life and he would be prevented from gloating that he killed me.

I began to pray.

I passed in and out of prayer, in and out of consciousness, and then I heard shouting down the hall. I heard my mother's voice.

"Break it down. Break the son of a bitch down. My baby's in there." Wood groaned, then splintered, and the door gave way. My little mother walked through the opening. She saw me and fainted. Later she told me that was the only time in her life she had done so.

The sight of my face swollen to twice its size and my teeth stuck into my lips was more than she could stand. So she fell. Three huge men followed her into the room. Two picked her up and she came to in their arms groggily. They brought her to my bed.

"Baby, baby, I'm so sorry." Each time she touched me, I flinched. "Call for an ambulance. I'll kill the bastard. I'm sorry."

She felt guilty like all mothers who blame themselves when terrible events happen to their children.

I could not speak or even touch her but I have never loved her more than at that moment, in that suffocating, stinking room.

She patted my face and stroked my arm.

"Baby, somebody's prayers were answered. No one knew how to find Mark, even Boyd Puccinelli. But Mark went to a mom-and-pop store to buy juice and two kids robbed a tobacco vendor's truck." She continued telling her story.

"When a police car turned the corner, the young boys threw the cartons of cigarettes into Mark's car. When he tried to get into his car, the police arrested him. They didn't believe his cries of innocence, so they took him to jail. He used his one phone call to telephone Boyd Puccinelli. Boyd answered the phone."

Mark said, "My name is Mark Jones. I live on Oak Street. I don't have any money with me now, but my landlady is holding a lot of my money. If you call her she will come down and bring whatever you charge."

Boyd asked, "What is your street name?"

Mark said, "I'm called Two Fingers Mark."

Boyd hung up and called my mother, giving her Mark's address. He asked if she would call the police. She said, "No, I'm going to call my pool hall and get some roughnecks, then I'm going to get my daughter."

She said that when she arrived at Mark's house, his landlady said she didn't know any Mark and anyway the guy hadn't been home for days.

Mother said maybe not, but she was looking for her daughter and she was in that house in Mark's room. Mother asked for Mark's room. The landlady said he kept his door locked. My mother said, "It will open today." The landlady threatened to call the police, and my mother said, "You can call for the cook, call for the baker, you may as well call for the undertaker."

When the woman pointed out Mark's room, my mother said to her helpers, "Break it down. Break the son of a bitch down."

In the hospital room I thought about the two young criminals who threw stolen cigarette cartons into a stranger's car.

How when he was arrested he called Boyd Puccinelli, who called my mother, who gathered three of the most daring men from her pool hall.

How they broke down the door of the room where I was being held. My life was saved. Was that event incident, coincident, accident, or answered prayer?

I believe my prayers were answered.

I recovered in Mother's house. Her friend Trumpet was bartending at the Sutter Street Bar. Mother said, "Trumpet just telephoned me. He knows I have a wanted out on Mark's ass, and Mark is drinking down there. Here is a piece." She offered me her .38 Special and I took it.

"Go to C. Kinds Hotel across the street from Sutter's. Telephone Mark from the lobby. Trumpet said he can keep Mark there for at least an hour. Telephone him and use a southern accent. Say you met him a few nights ago and you are at C. Kinds Hotel and would like to see him again. When he walks out of the bar, you step out of the hotel lobby. Walk to the corner and shoot him. Kill the bastard. I promise you will not do a day. He tried to kill you. Shoot him."

I telephoned from the hotel lobby. Mark did not recognize my voice. He flirted, asking me, "What's your name?"

I said, "Bernice. I'm in the lobby. Come over."

He laughed and said, "Right away."

In seconds he was on the corner and starting to cross the street.

I walked out of the lobby holding the gun. I saw him before he saw me. I had enough time to shoot, but I didn't want to do it. He was a few steps into the street before he saw me and the pistol in my hand.

"Maya, please don't kill me. God, please don't. I'm sorry. I love you."

I didn't feel sorry for him. I felt disgust. I said, "Go back in the bar, Mark. And go to the toilet. Go on. I won't shoot you."

He turned and ran.

My mother shook her head. "You didn't get that from me. That came from your Grandmother Henderson. I'd have shot him like a dog in the street. You are good, honey. You're a better woman than I am."

She wrapped me in her arms. "You never have to worry about him again. I put the news in the street. He knows if he ever walks the street in San Francisco, his ass is mine, and I won't hesitate."

My two jobs barely paid my bills. I began in a dinette at 5 A.M. as a fry cook and worked there until 11 A.M. The second job, in a Creole diner, went from 4 P.M. until 9 P.M.

In the hours between the breakfast job and the afternoon job, I would pick up Guy from school and take him to the allergist, where I was given a list of foods to buy to which he was not allergic. Guy was allergic to tomatoes, bread, milk, corn, and greens. When we left the allergist, we would stop at the Melrose Record Shop. He would head for the children's records and I would take the blues and bebop sides. Each of us would select a cubicle and listen to the music we had chosen.

After an hour or so, we would make our selections. I would pay for the records and then we would go home. I would have just enough time to see him safely in the house before I had to report to my evening job at the Creole kitchen.

One morning in the allergist office I picked up a slick women's magazine and began reading an article titled "Is Your Child Really Allergic or Is It Possible She's Not Getting Enough of Your Attention?"

Guy was finished with the allergist before I was done reading the article. I asked the receptionist if I could take the magazine and told her I would bring it back at our next appointment. When she said yes, I put it in my bag and didn't look at it until I finished my evening job. Back home I sat at the kitchen table and began to finish the article.

The piece infuriated me. I was about to throw the magazine in the trash when my mother telephoned. I answered abruptly.

She asked, "What is the matter?"

I said, "I am sick of white women."

My mother asked, "What have they done to you now?"

"It's not just me. It's just they think they know it all."

My mother said, "I'm on my way over there. Put some ice in a glass, please. I will bring my own Scotch."

I washed my face and brushed my hair and had the glass of ice ready when she rang the bell.

When she stepped in the door I was ready for her to say, "Sit down, I have something to say."

Instead she asked to see the article I was reading. I gave her the magazine and poured myself a glass of wine. When she finished reading, she smiled and said, "What is it that made you so angry?"

I said, "White women who have been white all their lives and are somewhat rich, have someone to pay all their bills, think that everybody is like them. I have to have two jobs and can hardly make it over and I am doing the best I can."

My mother said, "Sit down, I have something to say."

I had been expecting that and I sat down.

She said, "I know you are too proud to borrow and you would never beg, but here is the truth: You have a child who is not well and you have a mother who loves you. I do not want to lend you any money but I do want to invest a thousand dollars in your future. This is not a loan, nor is it a gift. This is an investment.

"I will expect you to start repaying me in three months. I expect you will be able to spend more time with your son. You must find another job that will pay well because I would like five percent interest on my money. I know you are fair and you know I am tough. Let's forget about the white women and just think about ourselves."

I thanked her for her offer and the next morning, when I gave notice for the fry cook job, the owner of the second restaurant also gave me notice.

Suddenly I had a large amount of money invested in me by my mother and no job. I walked Guy to school leisurely, rather than drop him off in a hurry as I did each morning. His happiness was contagious. I found myself giggling.

He jumped, danced, and held my hand, tore away again, and ran to the corner and then back again. His cheer almost made me weep.

When I picked him up at lunchtime, he insisted that I not walk on the cracks in the pavement. In fact, I had to jump as he jumped. I did so. His delight at seeing me jump made him giggle. His giggle tickled me and I jumped more and more.

In two weeks, the allergies, which had caused him to itch so bad he would scratch his skin until it bled, ceased being an aggravation. In four weeks, the allergy sores healed.

Fortune was smiling on me. I decided to help it along.

I applied for a job at the Melrose Record Shop

and was hired. The new job paid me a wondrous salary.

My mother said her friends told her that I had once been seen jumping on the street with my son and playing as if I were a child. She said, "No, she was not playing. She was just being a good mother."

*"Baby, I've been thinking and now I am sure. You are
the greatest woman I've ever met."*

16

David Rubinstein was a Reform Jew. Louise Cox was a Christian Scientist and I was a CME and Baptist believer. Amazingly we not only got along very well, we liked each other. The record shop was the most complete music shop in the black neighborhood in the Fillmore District.

Charlie Parker, Dizzy Gillespie, and Miles Davis ruled the bebop roost. Count Basie, Joe Williams, Ray Charles, Dinah Washington, Billy Eckstine, Nat King Cole, and Sarah Vaughan starred in the popular rhythm-and-blues music. The old-timey blues singers managed their own section of the collection.

I earned the title of knowing what musicians did what music and to what success, and as a result Dave and Louise gave me a raise before I expected it. I began paying Vivian Baxter back some of her money.

Tosh Angelos was so handsome and dignified that he took my breath away. He wore crewneck sweaters, tweed pants, and buckskin shoes. Also, he knew as much about jazz and bebop as I. After he chose a stack of records, he casually asked me my name and I told him. He bought a few records, paid for them, and left the shop.

Louise Cox said to me, "You really knocked his socks off."

I didn't think that was funny because I didn't think he had noticed me at all. Next week when he returned, he called me by my name and asked for more records. He played them, made his selection, paid for them, and left. On his third visit, Guy had been dropped off at the store. Tosh greeted me and asked if I was related to the five-year-old.

I said, "He is my son."

Tosh asked, "Does he like music?"

I said, "Yes."

He smiled and nodded and left the store.

I asked Louise what she knew about him.

"He is in the navy, of Greek descent, and is a graduate of the University of Oregon."

Weeks passed without any visit from Tosh. Louise said he might have gone out on the ship. I thought he might have found a better place to visit. After a few weeks, when I had given up on seeing him again, he entered the record shop in his naval uniform and asked if I would go out to dinner with him.

I said yes and that I would ask my aunt to look after Guy. He said that the next time we went out we would take Guy, but the first time he wanted me to himself.

On the first date Tosh blinded me with his brilliant wit and won my heart with his stories. The next four months the three of us or just Tosh and I visited every restaurant in the neighborhood and dined together. We played chess together, twenty questions, and parlor games.

We found we liked each other and because he made me and Guy laugh, I felt myself looking anxiously forward to his arrival. One evening after dinner and a humorous game of twenty questions, Guy went to bed. Tosh and I were sitting drinking wine. I invited him to stay over. He was as gentle and passionate as I could have hoped. Our relationship became more intense. I was delighted, but not surprised.

After a few weeks, he asked if I would marry him. I said I wanted to, but first I should speak to my mother. Mother had met Tosh on one of our evenings of parlor games and she had liked him, so when I told her I had something to say, she agreed to come to my house.

After Guy had gone to bed I told her of Tosh's proposal and that I had said yes. She was furious.

"How can you talk about marrying a white man?" she asked.

I said to her, "I thought you had no prejudices."

She said, "I don't, but if you are going to marry a white man, it is just as easy to fall in love with a rich one as it is with a poor ass."

I said, "I didn't ask how much money he had. I asked if he would love me, protect me, and help me raise my son."

She asked, "What did he say?"

I said, "He said yes!"

Vivian Baxter asked me, "And you believed him?"

I said, "Yes."

She asked, "What's going to happen to you? What the hell is he bringing you—the contempt of his people and the distrust of yours? That's a helluva wedding gift."

Of course, I was bringing him a mind crammed with a volatile mixture of insecurities and stubbornness, and a five-year-old son who had never known a father's discipline.

She asked me, "Do you love him?"

I didn't answer.

"Then tell me why you are going to marry him," she said.

Vivian Baxter appreciated honesty above all virtues.

I told her, "Because he asked me, Mother."

She nodded, said, "All right, all right," turned on her high heels, and strutted to the door. "Good luck."

The following week she called to tell me she was moving from San Francisco to Los Angeles. I asked Bailey to come over. I told him that Mother had broken my heart.

He said, "You have broken her heart. She thought you knew enough to stay alone or marry a rich man."

I said, "None came calling."

He said, "Well, she's going to move, but you have a brother and I will support you and I will call Tosh my brother."

17

Tosh and I did get married. My mother did move to Los Angeles. Tosh found a commodious house with three bedrooms, a formal dining room and living room, and a large kitchen. The three of us were very comfortable in the semi-furnished house. We shopped for a kitchen stove, a refrigerator, and sofas for the living room. While I loved being a housewife, my heart ached for my mother's presence.

Bailey gave me her phone number and I telephoned her once. She said, "You know that I love you and that I hope you will be happy. You also know that I am not a liar, so I would not tell you that I expect you to be happy with the husband you have chosen. But I do hope that you will not be totally miserable."

For the most part, I fitted into married life as a foot fits into a well-worn shoe. Tosh asked me to leave the job at the record store. He said too many men were flirting with me and he was jealous. I had no inkling that his jealousy would grow dangerous. In fact, since no one had ever shown me such desire, I was flattered. So, at his suggestion, I applied for a job at the Metropolitan Life Insurance Company. I was hired as a file clerk. I took a dance class twice a month and shopped Saturdays in the large supermarket aisles. I cooked dinner every day with my new pots and my brand-new stove.

We met some racially mixed couples and on Saturday nights, we sat in our living room playing twenty questions, charades, and drinking cheap wine. Tosh recognized that I missed my mother. He said, "I understand her. She doesn't like whites."

I swore that was not the truth.

He said, "She likes whites. She just doesn't want her daughter married to one."

Guy and Tosh made good friends. He taught Guy chess and I bought new cookbooks and began to experiment on fancy dishes. Bailey and his live-in love, Yvonne, came at least once a week. My marriage left me wanting only for two things: my relationship with my mother and my relationship with my God.

Tosh was an atheist. He had told me so while we were courting, but I was sure the Lord would help me change his mind. I was wrong. He said there was no God and that I was foolish to go to church. I was afraid that he would woo my son away from his religious teaching, and so whenever we were alone, I would tell Guy stories about Jesus and the miracles He had done. I taught him the beatitudes, the Lord's Prayer, and the Twenty-Third Psalm. When we were alone, I would test him on his memory. We would sing, "This little light of mine, I'm going to let it shine." I began an action which would become routine.

Then I decided to be unfaithful to Tosh by going to a nearby church. One Sunday after I had made breakfast I put on my exercise sweat suit and said I was going for a walk. I went to Bailey and Yvonne's house, where I had stashed Sunday clothes and shoes. At church the minister shouted and the people sang and I felt better having been in the house of the Lord. I returned to Yvonne and Bailey's house and changed back into my sweats and walked home. The fact that I had lied in no way diminished my sense of righteousness.

The marriage carriage was wheeling along. The bumps it encountered were caused by the facts that my mother never telephoned me and that twice a month I would steal off and go to church and lie about it.

One morning Bailey telephoned me to say that our mother was coming home and she would like to see me. At first I said no. I wanted to show her I could be as tough as she was, but the hope, the desire to see her beautiful face and hear her laughter was too great for me to refuse her a visit.

I asked Bailey if she would telephone me. The phone rang and she asked, "Baby, may I come to your house?"

I said, "Please do. Come to dinner on Sunday."

She asked, "Shall I come after church?"

I answered, "Yes."

I literally trembled with excitement. I knew she loved roast chicken with cornbread dressing and giblet gravy. I told Tosh and Guy that my mother was coming. Guy was happily excited.

Tosh asked, "Has she forgiven me for being white?"

I couldn't answer.

I bought a small bottle of Scotch and set the table. My mother arrived dressed elegantly as usual and she was accompanied by a nice-looking lady whom she introduced as Lottie Wells. She said Miss Wells was her close friend and a nurse and she would like me to think of her as my auntie.

My mother's smile was beautiful and so welcoming to my eyes that I forgot that she had abandoned me again. She held me for a long hug and when we broke our embrace her face was wet with tears.

She said, "Baby, please forgive me. I don't care if you marry a donkey; I will never walk off and leave you alone again. I have brought Lottie to meet you. I have told her so much about you and Guy and I want you all to get to know each other. You are both going to love her, I'm sure."

I was pleased to see Lottie's face and see her tears of joy.

I cried and the three of us embraced.

Guy came running down the hallway. "Grama, Grama!"

She kissed him and said, "My, how you have grown."

Tosh appeared. "Welcome," he said. "We've been waiting for you for a long time."

I know she could have said something sharp but I was very glad she didn't. We went into the living room and she sat looking around, appraising the room, the furniture, the décor.

I brought her and Aunt Lottie a Scotch and water; Tosh and I joined with wine. Guy had a glass of orange juice. We lifted the glasses to say skoal.

She said, "I have something to say. Ignorance is a terrible thing. It causes families to lose their center and causes people to lose their control. Ignorance knows no binds. Old people, young people, middle-aged, black, white, can all be ignorant. I thought my daughter was throwing herself away. She has already had a rough life and I thought she was willingly being stupid. Now I hear her beautiful voice and I see how happy Guy is and I appreciate your beautiful home. Please accept my apologies and my thanks to you, Tosh Angelos. I admire you for loving my darling daughter."

Dinner was a knockout.

*"Dancing liberated me and even made me feel
as if my body had a reason to be."*

(Maya Angelou, George Faison [of the Alvin Ailey American
Dance Theater], and Vivian Baxter at Maya Angelou's
Valley Road home, circa 1986)

18

When I was fifteen years old, I received a scholarship to attend the California Labor School. I studied dance there and it gave me a pleasure I had never known. Music urged my body to move and glide and lift and I followed its persuasion without resistance. I took free lessons as often as I could and when it was deemed that I had grown to an age where lessons had a price, I saved money stingily to afford rent, babysitter, food, records, and dance class. Sometimes I had enough money to take two classes in a month, and at other times, squeezing the eagle until it squawked, I managed to take one class a week.

I stopped dance class for the first few months of married life. My time was filled with learning the ways of my husband and watching the relationship that was developing between him and my son.

I returned to dance, spending only one evening per month. Tosh asked if he could visit the class. I welcomed him and he brought Guy along. I changed into a leotard and entered the classroom to see them sitting on folding chairs along the wall.

They waited until the class finished. We rode home together. Tosh said, "Obviously you are the best in the class—better than the teacher."

I was so pleased with the compliment.

For a few months, Tosh accepted the fact that I enjoyed dance. But I found he was less than happy one day when he said he wanted us to go to an Italian restaurant for dinner.

He was surprised when I told him I would not be free for dinner because I had signed up for a dance class. He asked if I was planning a career as a dancer. I said no, but told him the dancing liberated me and even made me feel as if my body had a reason to be. He assured me that that should never be my question. We both laughed at his insinuation and spoke no more about dance class.

Later, Tosh came out of the bathroom slamming the door behind him. I asked what was wrong. We had had no real arguments before. He said the towels were damp and there was no pleasure in trying to dry oneself with a damp towel. I told him we had dry towels and I would have brought him one if he had let me know. He said none of the towels were really dry because I didn't take the time to dry them properly. I said nothing but went to the linen closet and was shocked to find all the towels damp and on the floor.

I asked, "How did the towels get on the floor?"

He answered, "I put them there because they were not dry."

I said, "I had dried them myself."

He said, "You never had the time to be a proper housewife because you spent too much time in the dance studio."

I asked, "What do you want me to do?"

He was zipping his pants and buttoning his shirt. He said, "You are never going to be a professional dancer, so I don't understand why you're playing with dance. Guy and I need your attention and we deserve it."

I knew he had dampened the towels himself but I said nothing.

I waited two days and telephoned my mother.

She said, "Oh baby, I was going to telephone you. I'm not happy with the way my business is being run. Maybe you can help me. I'll be back in San Francisco this weekend and I would like to come to your house on Sunday, okay?"

When Mother arrived, she said, "As the old folk say, 'When the tabby is away, the rats will play.'" Her laughter held no joy.

She said, "I admit I was looking forward to coming home to see my baby and her baby, but when I heard how the rats were playing with my business, it became urgent that I come to San Francisco and right now."

Tosh said nothing. I asked, "How bad is it?"

She said, "Not unfixable. I'll light a fire under some butts and they'll be happy to leave, and I'll give a little more money to the rest and they'll be happy to stay."

Tosh just sat there. I asked more questions to keep the conversation going.

Mother looked at Tosh and stood up. She said, "I've got to go. I'll talk to you later."

Tosh waved a slight goodbye and I walked her to the door.

I said, "Mother . . ."

"I know, baby. I know he doesn't like me. I understand. I'd feel the same about him if he wasn't so good to you and Guy. Don't worry, I'll figure out a way for us to get along." Giving me a kiss, she walked out onto the steps.

Mother gave a big party to open her house. Guy and I attended. Tosh said he had another engagement. I realized Vivian Baxter was making every effort to be friendly to him, and he had no idea what that effort cost her.

I decided to ignore the fact that they didn't like each other, but silently I thanked my mother for her courtesy to him. Guy was doing well in school.

My job at the Metropolitan Life Insurance Company gave me a salary, but no pleasure. I had stopped the dance classes at the community center and had reduced my visits to the record shop. My days consisted of work, shopping, cooking, and playing parlor games with Guy and Tosh. I still slipped off to church when I could and I went to see my mother when she had time.

One day the telephone rang. Tosh was home and he answered. His voice became curt as he said, "Sure, sure, sure," then hung up. He came toward me and his face displayed displeasure. "That was your mother," he said. "She wants to pick us up and take us to the beach for drinks."

I said, "Great," but when I looked at his face I realized he didn't like my response. I tried to back up with "That would be nice."

He said, "She is bringing your Aunt Lottie to pick up Guy so it will just be the three of us."

Tosh knew he was going to be evaluated and he didn't have to like that, but I thought he shouldn't be surprised. Guy gladly climbed into Aunt Lottie's car. He knew that she would feed him milk shakes and hot dogs and anything else he asked for.

My mother drove us to the bar, which overlooked the shore where seals slid over and off the rocks. We lifted glasses and toasted each other, then my mother said, "I do not want to get into your business, but I am on Maya's side." She turned to me and said, "Baby, can you tell me why you are so unhappy?"

Tosh looked at me expecting me to deny being unhappy, but I thought about the question and realized that for the last few months I had always been near tears.

I said, "Most of the things I like have been taken away from me."

"Taken away or did you give them up?"

Tosh said defensively, "You said you wanted a home with a big kitchen and you have that. I am trying to be a good, faithful husband to you and a father to Guy. What else do you want?"

The two of them waited to hear what I would say and as I began to think about the dryness in my life, I couldn't hold back the tears.

"I have no friends. Tosh is jealous even of my friendship with Yvonne. He has stopped me from studying dance, he becomes angry if I stop at the record shop, and worst of all, I have to lie when I go to church."

Vivian exploded. "What?"

I said, "Whenever I can get away on Sunday, I go to Bailey and Yvonne's house and put on Sunday clothes and find some church not too far away, and enjoy the service. I put money in the collection and sometimes if I'm really carried away, I will write my name down and my phone number."

My mother's laugh was sardonic. She said, "You mean you have to lie to go to church?"

Tosh said, "I knew about it."

I asked, "Have you been following me?"

He denied that and added, "One evening when you were at the community center, I answered the telephone. A voice asked for Sister Antelope."

"I told them there is no Sister Antelope here."

The voice said, "I'm trying to reach Sister Maya Antelope. She joined church last Sunday and we have her scheduled to be baptized at the Crystal Pool Plunge on the first Sunday."

I asked, "You decided not to tell me?"

Tosh said, "You decided not to tell me?"

My mother looked at the two of us. "Is your relationship built on lies? Maybe you want to think about that. Let's drink up and I'll take you home."

Tosh asked, "Is that why you asked us out?"

"Ever since I've been home, I've seen that Maya has been sad enough to break down and cry. Now I understand."

Tosh asked, "And how can you fix that? Whose butt will you light a fire under?"

She said, "Are you ready? I'll pay the check."

Tosh said, "We'll call a cab."

I started to get up and follow her, but she said, "No, baby, you do what your husband wants you to do. But you have to think about the place that you are in."

I sat back down with Tosh as she walked to the cashier.

19

Mother and I were having coffee at the kitchen table when Tosh and seven-year-old Guy came in from a basketball game. I had prepared dinner and set the table. Mother told me she had an appointment so she wouldn't be staying. She greeted Tosh and Guy and said she'd like to take us out to dinner on Saturday night. She knew a Russian restaurant that served borscht and beef stroganoff. She was sure we would enjoy it.

Tosh thanked her for the invite but said he couldn't come. The tone of his voice told her he didn't want to come. My mother gave him a brisk "Okeydokey." She then gave me and Guy a kiss and left.

I asked, "Tosh, why can't you come to dinner— what will you be doing?"

"I think we're seeing too much of your mother."

I didn't respond because I didn't want to argue in front of Guy. That was not the whole truth. The whole truth was I didn't know what to say.

Guy and I went to dinner at the Russian restaurant and my mother never mentioned Tosh, but he was very present in his absence.

Guy asked, "Why didn't Dad come to dinner?"

My mother looked at him and at me, then asked, "When did Tosh start becoming his dad?"

I said, "They both decided."

"I see" (which meant she didn't see).

The light in my marriage waned as the sun sets in the western sky. At first the dimness is hardly noticeable, then noticeable but not alarming. Then with a rush, the light is vanquished by darkness. I realized I had lost interest in the marriage when I no longer wanted intimacy with my husband and no longer had concern about cooking exquisite meals. When music lost its talent to lighten my mood, I had to admit that what I wanted, I did not have. I wanted an apartment for myself and my son.

Tosh told me he understood when I explained that I missed my friends, the dance classes, and the freedom to mention God, Jesus, and faith without having a knock-down, drag-out argument. I disliked that he forced me to defend my basic beliefs.

Tosh took my departure with such equanimity

that I believe he was as relieved as I that our marriage had ended.

Guy was devastated at the news of our breakup and he blamed me. He remained angry for about a year and I found it impossible to explain to him that we had worn the marriage out. Bailey found it hard to understand why I had left the security of married life.

He thought he knew what I should have done. "All you had to do was make friends with Tosh's friends or bring people into your life and convince Tosh that they were his friends first."

Those were not solutions I was able to use.

Guy continued being distraught. Divorce in a family when the parents have been married a child's whole life can be painful. However, when the marriage is only three years old and the child has found his first father after four years of having none, divorce is a horror. At his young age, Guy thought that at last he could be like other children. At last he had a mother and a father who lived in the same house. At last he had someone who would answer out loud when he called "Dad."

After the separation we moved into a small two-bedroom apartment. My son cried himself to sleep so often and so piteously that I, too, wept alone in my bedroom.

I reported our situation to my mother, who never reminded me that she had said it wouldn't work out.

"It is normal," she said. "And although it is painful, imagine if you had allowed Tosh to take the sense of your person away. Guy would have lost the person he needs the most, his mother. For the sake of yourself, you must preserve yourself and for the sake of Guy, you must preserve his mother."

I looked for work, resumed dance class, and re-established my friendships at the Melrose Record Shop. My life was still teetering, and I was still searching for an even balance.

20

Nina (pronounced NINE-nah) was a strip-tease
dancer I had met in the dance class. She told me that
she wanted to be a serious dancer. In the meantime,
she made $300 a week stripping in a nightclub. She
heard that my marriage had ended and that I was job
hunting. She suggested that I try out at the club
where she worked. I sat in the dark rear of the Bonne
Nuit Dance Club and watched the women one after
another enter the stage and glide across the floor,
taking off pieces of apparel and making suggestive
movements with their hips and breasts. They stopped
after the brassieres were removed, leaving the nipples
covered with sequins. They patted their sequined
g-strings. They bowed to the loud and mostly male
audience and left the stage.

Because doing the strip-tease for me would be as
easy as chewing gum, I thought I should not refuse an
offer for a job out of hand. I knew I didn't want to be

known as a strip-tease dancer, but the prospect of three hundred dollars per week was also tantalizing. I called my mother and told her my dilemma.

She came to my new apartment. She said, "Let me make you a costume and you choreograph a dance. If you take a theme like Scheherazade, the Sultan's wife, you can use the music of Duke Ellington, 'Night in Morocco.' Understand if you are not going to take off your costume, what you wear will have to be so skimpy that the audience will be satisfied since they will be seeing nearly all of you. And there is this: You will not be posing onstage as you disrobe. You have to really be dancing."

Mother and I went to a theatrical costume shop. I bought g-strings and gauzy brassieres. We bought coke feathers, sequins, and bugle beads. My mother knew only a little more than I about sewing. We crowded the sequins, beads, and feathers onto the g-string and the brassiere.

I hired a conga drummer named Roy who played for the dance classes at the community center. I prepared for an audience at the Bonne Nuit Dance Club. Backstage I stripped and lathered my body with Max Factor #9 body makeup. I had no scars but the makeup made me feel theatrical. I put on the skimpy costume. Roy sat on a stool on the stage and at a cue, he began to play the conga drums.

Barefoot and nearly naked, I shouted, "Caravan!" and hit the floor. I began to dance sensuously, sultrily, and slowly. I allowed the music to pull me across the floor. I picked up the tempo and danced faster. Again I shouted, "Caravan!" I danced faster, shimmying and shaking and quivering. I slowed down. I had danced about ten minutes and slowed down again and again and returned to the slow, sensuous shimmer. In a large stage whisper, I said, "Caravan," and walked off the stage.

The owner gave me the job. He asked, "What is your name?"

I said, "Rita, the Dancing Señorita."

When I reported the outcome to my mother, she was pleased. She said, "I am not surprised. You are going far in this world, baby, because you dare to risk everything. That's what you have to do. You are prepared to do the best you know to do. And if you don't succeed, you also know all you have to do is try it again."

A few popular San Francisco columnists wrote about my performances at the Bonne Nuit Dance Club. The articles revealed my tactic with the customers. Strip-tease dancers and shake dancers were expected to coerce the customers into buying them drinks, pretending the drinks they ordered contained real alcohol. But I told the customers that if they bought me a single drink, I would be served quinine water or ginger ale and that I would also be given a portion or a fraction of the money they spent, but if they bought a bottle of poor champagne, a twenty-dollar bottle, I would be given five dollars for each bottle. The columnist added that I was also unique in another way—I could really dance.

San Franciscans started to drop in to the Bonne Nuit Dance Club. They crowded the place for the fifteen minutes of my set and would offer to buy me drinks. They would order the cheap champagne and turn their backs to the strip dancers. I had neither the sophistication nor the worldliness to make them think that I was clever. A group of men with one woman became regulars. The woman had long blond hair and smoked with a cigarette holder. She spoke as I thought Tallulah Bankhead would speak and the men wore expensive but casual clothes.

They were witty and easy to talk to. It is true that they laughed at me but they laughed at themselves as well. They invited me on my night off to visit the Purple Onion, which they owned and where Jorie Remus, the blond cigarette smoker in their group, was the star.

I told them I had a seven-year-old son and I spent my night off with him. Barry Drew and Don Curry, two of the owners, said I could bring Guy along. They would seat us in a corner. I began a routine once a week. Guy and I would go to dinner in a nice restaurant, catch the show at the Purple Onion, and then go home.

San Francisco was a center for entertainers who would become world-famous. People like Mort Sahl, Barbra Streisand, Phyllis Diller, the Kingston Trio, Josh White, Ketty Lester, and Odetta were among the singers and comedians who filled the bohemian nightclubs.

One evening I had been invited to dinner at Barry Drew's apartment. The conversation was heavy with sarcasm about folk singers.

I asked if they had heard calypso music and if they had, did they know that calypso was folk music. I reminded them that blues, spirituals, and gospel songs were all folk music. I sang a few bars of a calypso song I knew and they began to clap.

Jorie asked, "How many of those songs do you know?"

I said, "Lots."

She asked Barry, "Do you know what I'm thinking?"

Don, Barry, and all the rest shouted, "When you go to New York City, Maya should take your place at the Purple Onion!"

They told me I would be a stunning success and to begin planning for my debut.

I talked it over with my mother.

She asked how I felt about singing.

I admitted that I was nervous and that I had only sung in church.

She asked what would happen if I flopped.

"They will fire me."

My mother said, "They wouldn't be getting a cherry. You were looking for a job when you got the last one, and church is still there to sing in."

My friends brought in a coach, Lloyd Clark, to select songs and to choreograph movement for me. I rehearsed with a three-piece band and brought Guy down to every rehearsal. After four months dancing the hootchy-kootchy at the Bonne Nuit Dance Club, I opened as the star, singing calypso songs at the Purple Onion. I went from making $300 a week to $750 a week.

The publicity from the Purple Onion announced that the star, Maya Angelou, was a Watusi, born in Cuba, who sang calypso. My mother laughed until tears came down her cheeks. She said she never met a Watusi and had never been to Cuba, but she could swear that I was her daughter.

"I know what I'm talking about. I was there when you were born."

On opening night my mother, Aunt Lottie, my brother, Yvonne, and some new friends were there with Guy. My nerves were shattered. My mother and I had designed my dresses and had them made by one of her friends.

Tosh had told me that his name was originally Enistasious Angelopoulos and that when Greeks shortened their names, they would give an -os ending to the boys and the females would get an -ou ending. Although Tosh and I were separated, I kept the name Angelou because I liked the sound of it.

The Purple Onion was filled. Barry Drew, in his dramatic voice, said, "And now, Miss Maya Angelou from Havana, Cuba, will sing calypso."

Barefoot, in an exotic floor-length dress, I walked on the stage and began to sing "Run Joe." I had sung only two lines when my son joined from the back of the room, singing off-key and loudly. My mother, brother, Yvonne, Barry, and Don all rushed to Guy. My mother put her hand over his mouth. The audience laughed and I laughed. I asked the musicians to start again.

Mother's pride was evident. She brought her fellow members of the Women Elks Organization and the Order of the Eastern Star (African American secret women's organizations). She brought the merchant marines with whom she sailed and they made over me as if I were Lena Horne or Pearl Bailey.

Mother said, "Now you will see some of the world and you will show the world what you are working with." She laughed at her wit and I laughed at my imagined future.

21

A producer of *Porgy and Bess* telephoned me and offered me a job with the opera. He said the role of
Ruby, the girlfriend of Sportin' Life, was open and
because I could sing and dance, they wanted me to
play the role. I telephoned Mother and told her of
the offer. The problem was that the musical was pre-
paring to tour throughout Europe. I wanted to go
but I didn't want to leave Guy.

"You cannot turn down that chance to see Europe. Aunt Lottie and I will take care of Guy."

But I was afraid Guy would think I had gone off
and left him.

She said that sooner or later I would have to leave
him and that I could not keep him on my hip forever.
At least this time he would be left in good care.

I sat Guy down in the kitchen and explained I
would be away for a few months but he would stay

*"She was a raconteur and would entertain my friends
as if they were her friends."*

(Vivian Baxter, Julio Finn [a writer of jazz and blues], Maya Angelou,
Dolly McPherson [a very close sister-friend, and an
English professor at Wake Forest], 1985)

with his Grandma and Aunt Lottie, and I would send money every week so that he could have everything he needed. I told him he had to be grown-up like the little man he was.

A few weeks later, we both held back our tears as I gave my luggage to the taxi driver. I hugged Guy at the door. He then began to cry because he was already missing his mother.

I boarded the plane to New York with my luggage filled with my best clothes and enough guilt to last me a year.

Porgy and Bess boasted a cast with the top African American operatic voices. Leontyne Price, William Warfield, and Cab Calloway had already been featured in the company when I joined. The friends I made in the cast taught me more about music in six months than I had learned during my whole life. I became adept in French and Spanish and I sang every evening in European nightclubs after the opera curtain fell. I taught dance during the day in Paris, at the Habima Theater in Tel Aviv, Israel, and at the Rome Opera House in Italy.

I enjoyed myself but I also bruised my psyche with self-flagellation. On one hand I had earned a secure place in the theater world, but on the other hand, when I telephoned Guy in San Francisco, we would end our calls weeping and sobbing.

I knew that if I missed Guy as much as I did, he must be missing me more. I was old enough to know that I would be seeing him soon, but I knew he had to be thinking sometimes that he would never see his mother again. The years I had spent in Arkansas without my mother made me know how lost a child feels when a parent is missing.

Although I had flown over to join *Porgy and Bess,* guilt made me afraid to fly back. I thought how if the plane fell, my son would grow up saying, "I never knew my mother. She was an entertainer."

I took a ship from Naples to New York (nine days), and a train from New York to San Francisco (three days and three nights), before I finally arrived at Fulton Street. The reunion was greater than the drama in Russian novels. I wrapped my arms around Guy and he sobbed on my chest.

"I swear to you, I'll never leave you again. If I go, when I go, wherever I go, you'll go with me or I won't go."

He fell asleep in my arms. I picked him up and lowered him into his own bed.

22

After one week of living in the uppermost floor of my mother's big house, anxiety gripped me again. I became convinced it would be difficult if not impossible to raise a happy black boy in a racist society. One afternoon I was lying on the sofa in the upstairs living room when Guy walked through. "Hello, Mom." I looked at him and had the impulse to pick him up, open the window, and jump. I raised my voice and said, "Get out. Get out now. Get out of the house this minute. Go out in the front yard and don't come back, even if I call you."

I telephoned for a taxi, walked down the steps, and looked at Guy. I said, "Now you may go in and please stay until I return." I told the cabdriver to take me to Langley Porter Psychiatric Clinic. When I walked into the office, the receptionist asked if I had an appointment. I said, "No." She explained with a sad face, "We cannot see you unless you have an appointment." I said, "I must see someone. I am about to hurt myself and maybe someone else."

The receptionist spoke quickly on the telephone. She said to me, "Please go see Dr. Salsey, down the hall on the right, Room C." I opened the door of Room C and my hopes fell. There was a young white man behind a desk. He wore a Brooks Brothers suit and a button-down shirt and his face was calm with confidence. He welcomed me to a chair in front of his desk. I sat down and looked at him again and began to cry. How could this privileged young white man understand the heart of a black woman, who was sick with guilt because she left her little black son for others to raise? Each time I looked up at him the tears flooded my face. Each time he asked what was the matter and "How can I help you?" I was maddened by the helplessness of my situation. Finally I was able to compose myself enough to stand up, thank him, and leave. I thanked the receptionist and asked her if she could call me a taxi.

I went straight to my voice teacher, who was my mentor and the only person other than Bailey to whom I could speak openly. As I went up the stairs to Frederick Wilkerson's studio, I heard a student doing vocal exercise. Wilkie, as he was called, told me to go into the bedroom. "I am going to make you a drink." Leaving his student, he brought in a glass of Scotch, which I drank, although at the time I was not a drinker. The liquor put me to sleep. When I awakened and heard no voices from the studio I went in there.

Wilkie asked me, "What's wrong?"

I told him I was going crazy.

He asked again, "What's really wrong?" Upset that he had not heard me, I said, "I thought about killing myself today and killing Guy. I'm telling you I'm going crazy."

Wilkie said, "Sit down right at this table. Here is a yellow pad and a ballpoint pen. I want you to write down your blessings."

I said, "Wilkie, I don't want to talk about that. I'm telling you I am going crazy."

He said, "First write down that you heard me say 'write' and think of the millions of people all over the world who cannot hear a choir, or a symphony, or their own babies crying. Write down, 'I can hear— Thank God.' Then write down that you can see this yellow pad, and think of the millions of people around the world who cannot see a waterfall, or flowers blooming, or their lover's face. Write, 'I can see— Thank God.' Then write down that you can read. Think of the millions of people around the world who cannot read the news of the day, or a letter from home, a stop sign on a busy street, or . . ."

I followed Wilkie's orders and when I reached the last line on the first page of the yellow pad, the agent of madness was routed.

I picked up the pen and began.

I can hear.
I can speak.
I have a son.
I have a mother.
I have a brother.
I can dance.
I can sing.
I can cook.
I can read.
I can write.

When I reached the end of the page I began to feel silly. I was alive and healthy. What on earth did I have to complain about? For two months in Rome I had said that all I wanted was to be with my son. And now I could hug and kiss him anytime the need arose. What the hell was I whining about?

Wilkie said, "Now write, 'I am blessed. And I am grateful.'"

After that exercise, the ship of my life might or might not be sailing on calm seas. The challenging days of my existence might or might not be bright and promising. From that encounter on, whether my days are stormy or sunny and if my nights are glorious or lonely, I maintain an attitude of gratitude. If pessimism insists on occupying my thoughts, I remember there is always tomorrow. Today I am blessed.

*"I will put my foot in their door up to my hip until
every woman can get in that union, and can get
aboard a ship and go to sea."*

(Auckland, New Zealand, 1975)

23

In Los Angeles, I began singing in the nightclub Cosmos Alley. I met the great poet Langston Hughes, and John Killens the novelist. I told them I was a poet and wanted to write. "Why don't you come to New York?" John Killens asked. He added, "Come find out if you really are a writer."

I considered the invitation seriously.

I thought, My son is sixteen. We could just move to New York. That would be good, and I would become a writer. I was young enough and silly enough to think that if I had said so, it would be so.

I called my mother. "I am going to go to New York and I would love you to meet me in Bakersfield or Fresno. I just want to be with you a little bit before I leave the West Coast."

She said, "Oh baby, I want to see you, too, because I'm going to sea."

"To see what?"

"I'm going to become a seaman."

I asked, "Why, Mother?" She had a real estate license, she had been a nurse, and she owned a gambling house and a hotel. "Why do you want to go to sea?"

"Because they told me they wouldn't let any woman in their union. They suggested that the union certainly would not accept a Negro woman. I told them, 'You want to bet?' I will put my foot in their door up to my hip until every woman can get in that union, and can get aboard a ship and go to sea."

I didn't question that she would do exactly what she said she would do. We met a few days later in Fresno, California, at a newly integrated hotel. She and I pulled into the parking lot at almost the same time. I brought my suitcase and Mother said, "Put it down, beside my car. Put it down. Now come on."

We went inside the lobby. Even in this newly integrated hotel people were literally amazed to see two black women walking in. My mother asked, "Where's the bellcap?" Someone stepped up to her. She said, "My daughter's bag and my bags are outside beside the black Dodge. Bring them in, please." I followed as she walked to the desk and said to the clerk, "I am Mrs. Jackson and this is my daughter, Miss Johnson, and we have reserved rooms."

The clerk stared at us as if we were wild things

138

from the forest. He looked at his book and found that we did indeed have reservations. My mother took the keys he offered and followed the bellman with the bags to the elevator.

Upstairs we stopped in front of a door and she said, "You can leave my baggage here with my baby's." She tipped the man.

She opened her bag and lying on top of her clothes was a .38 revolver. She said, "If they were not ready for integration, I was ready to show it to them. Baby, you try to be ready for every situation you run into. Don't do anything that you think is wrong. Just do what you think is right, and then be ready to back it up even with your life. Make sure that everything you say is two-time talk. That means say it in the closet and be prepared to say it on the city hall steps, and give anybody twenty minutes to draw a crowd. Don't do it to make news. Do it to make it known that your name is your bond, and you are always ready to back up your name. Not every negative situation can be solved with a threat of violence. Trust your brain to suggest a solution, then have the courage to follow through."

The implied challenge in the saying "If you can make it in New York, you can make it anywhere" did not intimidate me or my son. However, we did move to Brooklyn, not Manhattan. I found a two-bedroom house in Brooklyn and Guy went to the high school nearby. I sang in a nightclub in Manhattan and Guy got an after-school job in a bakery in Brooklyn. He gave me a portion of his salary and a portion of the baked goods he was given and we were living high on the hog. I began writing songs with Abbey Lincoln and Max Roach and joined the Harlem Writers Guild.

Escorts were plentiful and satisfying. To keep Guy's respect, however, I never allowed anyone to stay overnight. If I stayed overnight with a friend, I always managed to be home before daybreak. I was learning to write, thanks to the encouragement and guidance of the members of the Harlem Writers Guild.

After I had lived in Brooklyn for a year I felt that I was up to facing New York City head-on. When an apartment became available on Central Park West, I rented it. Guy and I and some friends piled our furniture up on a moving van and transferred into the heart of the city that never sleeps. Once I was settled in New York, my mother came to visit. I gave a dinner for her. She approved of my apartment and my friends. She went to Guy's school and met the prin-

cipal and was satisfied that he was in the right place at
the right time.

After I had been a guest on Bill Moyers's televi-
sion program, I, along with Rosa Guy and my
mother, was invited to a party at his home in Long
Island. My mother and I got into the limo that pulled
up outside my apartment. We introduced ourselves to
the passenger who was already in the car. He was an
employee of Moyers's station. The limo took us to
Rosa Guy's building on Riverside Drive. The apartment house had known elegance in its younger days,
but drug sellers and buyers occupied the apartment
house across the street from Rosa's building, and the
finery that had been in her lobby had disappeared.
The rugs and the sofas had been stolen and the mail-
box vandalized.

When the limo pulled up in front of the building,
Mother asked, "What is Rosa's apartment number?
I'll go to get her." She told our seat partner to come
with her.

I said, "No, Mother, I will go. You stay here."

She said firmly, "No, no, I will go. I said I will go
in." To the man in the seat beside me she said again,
"You come with me."

I think he was more afraid of Mother than the
ominous apartment building in Harlem. They en-

tered the shabby lobby and found the elevator. When they boarded the elevator, Mother pushed the button for the sixth floor but the elevator went to the basement. The door opened and a man entered the elevator and looked at the little black woman and little white man and asked, "How far are you going?"

My mother patted her purse and said, "I'm going all the way. I came here to go all the way. How far are you going?"

The man got off the elevator on the first floor.

24

Porgy and Bess was going to be made into a movie with Diahann Carroll as Bess and Sidney Poitier as Porgy.

Otto Preminger was the director, and when he saw that I was six feet tall and Sammy Davis Jr., who was playing Sportin' Life, was about five three or four, he asked Hermes Pan, the choreographer, to create a dance for us.

During the shooting of the film in California I made friends with Nichelle Nichols, the actress who was later to become Lt. Uhura on *Star Trek*. Her gentleman friend and my gentleman friend were buddies and since we had a long weekend, and we were near San Francisco, I invited them to come down to San Francisco, where I had grown up, and to allow me to show off my city. They accepted my invitation.

I telephoned Mother and said I wanted to bring

three people down to introduce them to her and that we were going to "do" San Francisco.

"Oh baby, do honey, do come. Come home first. Come."

We arrived at my mother's house on Fulton Street. After all the introductions, she gave us drinks. As we went out to have a good time my mom said, "Come back around two thirty, no later than, and I will make you some omelets or crepe suzettes. Just come back and tell me all the fun you had."

We had a big wonderful San Francisco time and we did come back to Mother, who had her omelet pans out and a cold bottle of champagne. We had an after-theater dinner with her. My mother showed Nichelle and her gent where they could stay and she told my fella where he could stay, then she asked me, "Baby, will you stay with me?"

I said, "Of course."

"I have run you a bath."

I enjoyed the bath, and when I got to her bedroom she was already in her nightgown. I joined her in the bed and she said to me, "Baby, telephone this number and ask for Mr. Thomas, and say it's long distance. Ask for Mr. Cliff Thomas."

I dialed the number and a woman's voice said, "Yes?"

I said, "Good morning, this is long distance for Mr. Cliff Thomas."

The voice began yelling. "Bitch you know this is not long distance!" I hung up the telephone. "Mother, the woman said . . ." I repeated the woman's statement.

"That son of a bitch, he's over there with his wife."

"Where else should he be?"

"No, they have been separated three years, and he and I have been together at least two years. Now I know he is trying to get back with her. I have asked him, 'Do you want to go back with her? Don't lie to me; do you want to go back?' He said, 'No, no.' Yesterday I drove by her house and his car was parked in her driveway. I want to know what he is doing over there and why he is lying to me."

I said, "Oh Mom. Come, Mom, don't worry." I put my arms around her and stroked her shoulders. "You know it's all right. I know you will work it out. Calm down." I kept murmuring to her and I put myself to sleep.

A man's deep voice awakened me. "Thank you, Miss Myra. Oooh, thank you, Miss Myra, oohhhh." The man was crying, "Oooohhh, thank you, Miss Myra."

I sat up in the bed and there was a huge man kneeling at the foot of the bed and my mother standing there with her hand in a paper sack. The man was crying. He had urinated all over himself and probably even gone further, judging by the stench in the room.

"Mister get up. Get up and leave. Go."

"Oohhhhhh, thank you, Miss Myra." He stood up and rushed to the door. I took the paper sack.

Mother had her German Luger pistol in it. "Mother, what are you doing?"

"Oh baby, you don't know how they treat me."

"Well, they don't treat you that way very long, obviously."

"You know, he was over there, just as I suspected, with his wife."

"But Mother, how did you get him to come here?"

"Well, after you went to sleep, I got up and I took another bath and lotioned myself and I put on some clothes. And then I didn't have anything else to do, so I got my keys and got in my car and drove to her house. I rang the bell. And when his wife opened the door I put my pistol on her and I said, 'I'm here for your husband.'

"She said, 'Here he is.'

"I told him, 'Go, get in the driver's seat and let me show you why you are alive this morning.'"

She made him drive her back to her house. She told him, "Come on inside. Open the bedroom door and get on your knees because if it wasn't for my baby, I'd blow you a brand-new one this morning."

When he left I said to my mother, "You know I brought friends here. They think I am so such-a-much and they are in the house because I invited them. Nichelle Nichols and her fella and my fella, who are quite well-known artists, even famous, were going to be involved in a shooting. Was that fair to me?"

She came around to me and she said, "Baby, you know I didn't do anything to that man. He's the one who did something to me. You see, baby, you have to protect yourself. If you don't protect yourself, you look like a fool asking somebody else to protect you." I thought about that for a second. She was right. A woman needs to support herself before she asks anyone else to support her.

Maybe she could have found another time to assert herself and her rights than a night when my illustrious friends were in the house. But she didn't, and that was Vivian Baxter.

Years later a friend took me to have my hair done around 10 A.M. in a salon on Fillmore Street. The

147

beautician was busy and asked if I would come back in about an hour. There was an open bar across the street; after all, it was San Francisco. My friend and I went over to the bar. The bartender seemed familiar. After we ordered drinks I asked my friend Jim, "Will you ask the bartender his name?"

Jim asked the barkeep, "Excuse me, what is your name?"

"My name is Cliff." Then he looked at me. "Ask her if she knows me. I know her mother."

Then he spoke directly to me. "How's your mother, baby?"

I said, "She's fine, thank you."

He said, "I was just up in Stockton visiting her. She is sure one hell of a woman." He should know.

25

Lady bonded with a few friends from the Women Elks Organization, the members of the Order of the Eastern Star, and the Older Women's League (OWL) and formed a group she called the Stockton Black Women for Humanity.

She had included some of her white sister friends, one judge, one seamstress who sold exquisite fashions, and two nurses. She called them "honorary black women." They all collected clothes which they sent to the cleaners to be cleaned and others to be washed.

She used one of her garages as a closet, arranging clothes in sizes and colors. There were women's pants, summer house dresses, and formal Sunday clothes. Men's work pants and shirts, slacks, and dress shirts had their own space. Boys' and girls' clothes were arranged according to size.

The Stockton Black Women for Humanity gave

*Saturday, March 4, 1995, at the groundbreaking ceremony
for the Vivian "Lady B" Baxter Park in Stockton, California.
Vice Mayor Floyd Weaver is introducing Maya Angelou before
presenting the plaque for the park, with her grandson,
Colin Johnson, in the background.*

*"[Bailey] adored our mother, and laughing and joking, he
showed his delight at being with her."*

(Right to left: Vice Mayor Floyd Weaver, Colin Johnson, Maya Angelou,
Bailey Johnson [brother of Maya Angelou])

scholarships of $350 to students as they finished the eleventh grade. My mother said many students dropped out after the eleventh grade in high school because they didn't have the popular clothes to wear into their senior year of high school. The scholarships were given as money and gift cards for students to use at Sears and J.C. Penney department stores.

I went to visit Mother in her Stockton home one afternoon. She was in a mood of such hilarity she couldn't stop laughing. When I asked what was so funny, she said a month earlier the mayor of a nearby town had telephoned her and said, "Lady Baxter, we know you are famous for knowing everybody in Stockton and for being kind and generous to everybody. I am the mayor of this town and we have a situation here that I have not been able to improve."

The caller went on, "There is a man and woman, their teenage children, and his mother all living in a car. They have been seeking employment for two weeks to no avail. I wonder if I sent them to you, could you help them at all? They are all healthy and willing to work."

Mother asked, "How long have they been sleeping in the car?"

The mayor said, "For over a week."

Mother told her, "All right, let them sleep tonight in the car but here is my address. Have them come to my house tomorrow morning by seven A.M. I'll do my best."

The next morning the family arrived and Lady sent them to the garage to find clean clothes, gave them towels, and sent them off to shower, clean up, and dress.

When the family returned, Mother cooked a large breakfast and they ate heartily. Lady had called her friends and sent their clothes to the laundry and found jobs in supermarkets bagging groceries and jobs in gas stations and in parking lots. Before night-fall she had found accommodations for the family.

Weeks had passed and the mayor called my mother the day before I arrived. She said, "Lady Bax-ter, thank you very much for what you did for that family I sent to you. I'm in Stockton and if you have some coffee, I would love to come and have a cup of coffee with you."

My mother said, "Come."

A few minutes later her doorbell rang and she opened the door and a middle-aged white woman said to my mother, "I'm looking for Lady Baxter."

Vivian Baxter said, "You're looking at her."

When Mother told me that, laughing out loud, she said the mayor looked at her and almost shat. She expected her to be white. The mayor was white and the family she sent to my mother was white. She didn't understand that Stockton Black Women for Humanity were gathered to serve all humanity: white, black, Spanish-speaking, and Asian; fat, thin, pretty, plain, rich, poor, gay, and straight.

Mother said, "The mayor sat down and drank a half cup of coffee. She was so uncomfortable she said she had to go. I saw her to the door and the Lord knows, I felt sorry for her."

26

Mother telephoned. Her voice did not have its usual strength. "I need to see you. Can you come to San Francisco for a week? I'll help with the airline ticket."

I didn't need money, but I did want to know why the urgency, "Are you sick?"

"Yes, but I'm seeing a doctor and all will be well."

"I'll be there tomorrow."

"When you get into San Francisco, don't go home. I'm staying with a sick woman."

"You are not well and you're nursing someone else?"

"Yes, but I will leave here at the end of the week. Come on, honey, you'll understand when you get here."

That next evening I picked up a taxi from the San Francisco airport and told the driver to take me to the Stonestown Apartments. Immediately I knew my mother's patient was a white woman. I had not heard of any African Americans living in those apartments.

Mother met me as I stepped out of the elevator. A smile wrapped around her whole face. She was so happy to see me, she glowed. She took my bag and brought me into the apartment. We sat on the side of her bed and she patted my face and my leg. She didn't look very strong, but whatever was ailing her had taken only a little of her spirit.

"Don't worry, I'm not that sick, but I need to get my property straightened out. Your brother is coming in tomorrow from Hawaii."

Things were more serious than I thought, or than she was letting on.

I asked her about the woman she was working for. She said the woman had three nurses and they worked three days and nights. There were maids who worked eight-hour shifts, but the nurses worked around the clock. This was the first of my mother's three days.

I asked what was wrong with her employer. She said, "Nothing medical, really, but she has forgotten almost all of her past. She remembers a few things from her childhood, but everything else is gone. She thinks I am her older sister and she's about eighty years old. She is white, has a little accent, but I think she's American."

Mother went to the kitchen and made me a sandwich. She brought it and we had a glass of wine at the table. As we ate she said that when I got up the next day, after my shower, I should come down the hall to the living room. She had told the maid that I was coming, so I was to simply greet her with "Hello, Miss Susan."

I awakened a little fuzzily the next morning; maybe it was the amount of alcohol I drank or the jet lag left rocking in my shoes.

I walked down the hall and saw my mother's white shoes and stockings sticking out. Mother was sitting on the sofa and as I got closer, I saw a little woman sitting on the sofa opposite my mother. A wild splash of color over her head made it seem as if the wall had gone crazy. I gasped. My mother jumped up and came to me. She took my hands. "What on earth is it?" she asked. When I turned to my mother, the area over her head also seemed to be colors gone mad, screaming. I had never had such an experience like that in my life. I was shaken. My mother held me. "What's the matter? What's the matter?"

I couldn't talk.

The little white woman came over and took my hand. In a whispery voice she said, "Hello, dear. I know who you are. You are my sister's daughter. She told me you were coming. You are Vivian's daughter." She patted my cheek. I pulled away and thought I really had lost it.

Tears slipped down my face and I didn't know why. My mother didn't know, either, but the little woman said, "Oh, of course I know why she's crying. It's because of the Matisses." I looked at her and then I looked over her head and there was a Matisse, about seven feet by seven, and another equally large one over the sofa where my mother had sat. All the colors, all the action, in such a narrow space, were more than I could take.

The woman said, "These are just Matisses. Come, my dear, come. Oh Vivian, don't be afraid, she's all right. It's just the power of Henri's work."

The woman took my hand, and although I was shaking, I allowed her to guide me around her apartment. She had original paintings by Picasso, Matisse, Rouault; large, great pieces adorned the wall in the small San Francisco apartment. She even had a small bust of a man. She patted it and said, "This is Leo. He wants to marry me. He's nice. He comes over here and I like him enough, but I haven't said yes. Picasso made this for me. It's a bust of Leo."

I returned to my mother's bedroom and thought about what I had just experienced. I had had a physical response to art. I breathed deeply and was relieved. For the first time in my life art seemed to have a tonal quality. I could almost hear the art as if it were a great chord of a symphonic piece.

When I finally achieved some balance, I went to sit in the kitchen. Mother joined me. She introduced me to Mrs. Stein, who also sat down with us. Mrs. Stein explained to my mother that sometimes artists respond in very strange ways when they see the work of other artists.

"Your daughter cried because she is an artist, and she's my niece and naturally she's very, very sensitive."

I thought of the irony of the woman who had forgotten major portions of her life. She had forgotten that she had been married to one man for over fifty years . . . but she remembered the art.

I stayed there with my mom for two days. Then I went over to my mother's house and waited for her.

When she arrived she explained to me that Mrs. Stein was the widow of Leo Stein, who was the brother of Gertrude Stein. They had lived in Paris and collected great art in the early part of the twentieth century. Mr. and Mrs. Stein had come back to San Francisco, where he died.

Her family had taken an apartment for their mother. All the employees hired to look after her were carefully selected and bonded. Mrs. Stein, in her generosity and lack of memory, was apt to give pieces of art to her employees, who were informed to telephone the estate executor and report the gift. The executor would have the art picked up and put away. But her family let the rest of the art remain with her until she gave it away.

My mother said that was the expression of intelligence and love. Mrs. Stein's family knew that the art on the walls was more real to her than they themselves. Its presence in the apartment gave her assurance that she existed and that her existence was important.

27

Winter in Stockholm is hardly bearable. The cold assails the body and the darkness assaults the soul. The sun rises in the winter or attempts to rise at least by 10 A.M. By three in the afternoon it returns shamefully to the dark, and it rests there until the next morning, around ten, when it tries again to shine.

I was in Stockholm because a screenplay of mine was being shot there. The music I was writing for the screenplay was to be recorded in the Swedish Radio studios.

The stars of the film were well-known American stage actors, and a couple of movie actors were also in the cast.

The play was about an African American nightclub singer who was the toast of Europe. I based her character on the personality of Eartha Kitt. The actress who played the role was not a singer, so I wrote music for her that she could simply speak on pitch, much as Rex Harrison had spoken his lines in *My Fair Lady.* The actress came to my apartment in New York City to thank me. She thanked me for making it possible for her to take the lead because I had written simple music that she didn't have to sing. I had also written a character role for the actor Roscoe Lee Browne, but it had to go to another actor because Browne was making a film, starring John Wayne.

I went to Stockholm to meet the director and film crew. I was sitting in my hotel lobby when a young African American man saw me and ran over. He got down on his knees. "Maya Angelou, you are really so great. You really are our Shakespeare, and I thank you for this chance. I am going to do it well and you are going to be proud of me."

I said to him, "Don't kneel, please. Sometimes people put people on pedestals so they can see them more clearly and knock them off more easily. Get up."

"No, I want you to know I think you are our Shakespeare."

I said, "Oh, please don't. If you stay on your knees, I will get down there and if you lie out prone, I will lie down on the rug." Fortunately he believed me and got up.

The cast and crew had gathered. A Swedish director had been chosen. I accompanied him in the search for locations. The shooting began. The star, as written, was a true glamour queen. Her makeup was professionally applied and the luxuriant wigs she wore floated around her face. As the story progressed, from time to time she would remove the wig. She was quite wonderful to look at. Beneath her wigs, her hair was in braided cornrows, a style often worn by African American women. None of the Swedish beauticians knew how to plait cornrows. I was obliged to go to the set on early mornings to braid the star's hair. I appreciated the opportunity, since I could see how films were made. I developed a new ambition. I wanted to direct a movie. Every day I went to the location eager to learn more.

By the third week I began to understand about the setting up of lights and I saw how cameras could be switched to cover scenes. In 1972, I didn't know anyplace in the United States where a forty-year-old black woman could learn filmmaking and I was happy that I had happened upon my chance.

At the beginning of the fourth week, the star told the director that when I was on the set she got nervous. She couldn't act if she was nervous. Sorry, but she didn't want me on the set. The director, who, I gathered, had never before even shaken a black person's hand, must have felt caught between the Mississippi and the North Sea. He took the easy way out and asked me to come to the set only to braid her hair and then leave.

The next week, the actor who was playing the role I had written for Roscoe Lee Browne decided he had to return to New York. He was going home because he claimed the company had supplied real jewelry for the star and they had only given him zircons. He said he didn't come to Sweden to be treated like a second-class citizen. I went to his hotel and found him in his suite with a number of Swedish friends. His packed bags were in the hall.

I spoke to him. "Please, what are you doing? You realize we have shot four weeks. This is the first time that any black woman has ever had a screenplay done by a major company. We can't afford to send for another actor to come for that role. You said you wanted to do it."

"Who in the hell do you think you are, Shakespeare?"

I lowered my voice. "May I speak to you in your bedroom?"

He lifted his eyes, screwed up his face, mugging for his friends, and then agreed to come into the bedroom. As soon as I closed the door I knelt. "I am doing something very dangerous. I have gotten on my knees to you." I said, "Please, I beg you to consider." He told me what I could do to myself, which was a sexual impossibility.

I stood up and became Vivian Baxter. I said, "Thank you for that, you silly ass! Now I will stay up all night and all day, and I will rewrite the rest of your role out of the script. I will have you run over by a Swedish bus. I promise you I will make the audience applaud when you die."

He sobered quickly. "Listen, I didn't mean that, Maya. I just wanted to see how serious you were about wanting me." He went out into the hall and got his bags and brought them back in.

I went back to my hotel and called my mother. I didn't use "Lady" or "Mother." "Mom, I need mothering. If you have ever done any, I need it now. I am sending you a check, and as soon as you get it please book a flight and come to Stockholm."

She said, "Baby, if any plane is leaving San Francisco today for Sweden, I will be on it. You pick me up tomorrow morning at the Stockholm airport."

I knew that if she said she was coming, she was coming. At eleven o'clock I asked Jack Jordan, one of the film's producers, to accompany me to the Stockholm airport. We went to the airport bar and while we waited, we drank and drank, until finally Jack had to be sent back to his hotel.

I sat at the airport waiting for my mother to mother me. The plane arrived at last and I went to the area where I could see my little mother come down the steps, tipping in her high-heeled shoes. She was in her typical Vivian Baxter dress, carrying her sable stole, and her sparkling diamonds were flashing. I waved at her and she waved back with a little military salute. As soon as she was through security, we embraced.

"Let me get your bags."

"No. Have somebody pick them up and keep them for us. You take me to the bar. I see you know where it is." So, of course, I took her to the bar. My mother said to the bartender, "Give my daughter a Scotch and water, whether she needs it or not. I will also have a Scotch and water. You have whatever you like, and give everybody in this place a drink."

My smart, glamorous, sophisticated mother sat back in her stool. As usual she was in charge. She turned around and faced me directly. "Baby, let me tell you something: A horse needs a tail more than one season." What on earth did that mean? I sent for her because I needed her desperately and she arrived with this completely befuddling wisdom. I asked, "Please say that again."

"A horse needs a tail more than one season. You see, a horse that thinks once summer is over it can get rid of the appendage stuck on the back of its butt, which it doesn't even have to look at, is a damned fool. If the horse lives, spring will come and the flies will be back, and the flies will begin worrying the horse. When the flies aggravate the horse's eyes and the ears, the horse would give anything for just a minute's peace.

"Baby, now they are treating you as if you are a horse's ass. Let me tell you something. All you have to do is get your work done. If these people live, they will come back to you. They may have forgotten how badly they treated you, or they may pretend that they have forgotten. But watch: They will come back to you. In the meantime, Mother is here. I will look after you and I will look after anybody you say needs to be looked after, any way you say. I am here. I brought my whole self to you. I am your mother."

I sublet an apartment so that we could be comfortable. My mother stayed with me for the entire shooting of the movie.

Each morning I went to the location to braid the star's hair. And each morning, until I finished, the crew would hold up action. They would not hang lights nor arrange cameras. The director and the actors stood together in silence until I left. For the first few days after Mother's arrival, I used all my control to hold back the tears. Slowly, I allowed my mother's presence to strengthen me. And as I crossed the little lawn adjacent to our building, I would see my mother standing in the window with a cup in her hand and a big smile on her face. I would take the glass elevator up to her floor, and my mother would greet me with a steaming hot cup of coffee.

She said the same thing every morning, "Hi, baby, come in. Here's some coffee and a kiss for you." Having her there kissing me, offering me coffee, made me feel like a little girl, like allowing me to sit in her lap. She stroked my shoulders and stroked my back and murmured to me. I stopped feeling sorry for myself.

Mother learned where the shops were. Sometimes she would ask me to accompany her. She found her way around the area. She asked if there were any likable cast members. When I said yes, she said I could invite them.

My mother made fried chicken, mashed potatoes, greens, cabbage, or kale. She would always buy a dessert. The bar was always stocked. She was a raconteur and would entertain my friends as if they were her friends. My mother was irresistible (when she wanted to be) and everyone fell in love with her when she wanted them to.

I noticed after a while, on the set, people started treating me differently. At first it was a little off-putting. The star began to smile more frequently at me when I was braiding her hair. The man who had threatened to run away, to leave us in a lurch, was back saying what a great writer I was and how honored he was. I began to wonder what made them change. I had not done anything unusual for them. Their salaries had not been increased, and the time they owed to the shooting of the film had not been decreased.

One morning as I was leaving, the director said I didn't have to leave the set anymore. What happened? Why did they change their ways of treating me? I came to the realization that it was because I had a mother. My mother spoke highly of me, and to me. But more important, whether they met her or simply heard about her, she was there with me. She had my back, supported me. This is the role of the mother, and in that visit I really saw clearly, and for the first time, why a mother is really important. Not just because she feeds and also loves and cuddles and even mollycoddles a child, but because in an interesting and maybe an eerie and unworldly way, she stands in the gap. She stands between the unknown and the known. In Stockholm, my mother shed her protective love down around me and without knowing why people sensed that I had value.

I never stayed at the shoot after I finished braiding the star's hair. I counted on luck giving me another chance to learn moviemaking.

Mother understood. She said, "You're my daughter. Don't take tea for the fever. You are your own woman."

After we wrapped the music, I began to think about my mother as a seaman. She had shipped from San Francisco to Hawaii to Tahiti, to Bora-Bora and on to New Zealand. She knew the Pacific but she had no knowledge of Europe. I asked her if she would come with me to Paris and then to London, and maybe sail the Atlantic back to New York City. She said she would be delighted. The thought of taking my mother to Europe somehow liberated me from my fear of flying.

I found a flight that left Stockholm for Paris and came with a one-week stay at a modest hotel. We would spend a few days in Paris and go on to London, then sail back to New York. From there Mother would continue on to California.

We said our farewells to friends in Stockholm and boarded the plane. We were both smokers at the time, so we sat in that section. The doors closed and the plane took off. I noticed that no one said, "Welcome, ladies and gentlemen. We are now closing the doors." I thought, Maybe this is how Swedish airlines do things. We were aloft when screens dropped from the ceiling. They informed passengers, "Smoking," "No Smoking," but still no one spoke.

We had been aloft about ten minutes when two cabin attendants came bowing down the aisle. When the signboards receded into the ceiling and the attendants began to speak in sign language, my mother and I looked at each other and at the same moment realized that we had gotten onto a plane full of deaf people. We were amazed and started laughing.

When the attendants came by, my mother said, "Excuse me."

Shocked, the cabin attendant said, "You're talking!"

Mother said, "Oh yes, and I'm listening, too."

The attendant hurried away without finding out what my mother wanted. She told the other cabin attendants that two of us were talkers. I supposed she alerted them so they would not be too shocked.

My mother and I ordered drinks and had a very nice time laughing and smoking, enjoying each other. When we arrived in Paris, we disembarked from the plane and a uniformed attendant began communicating in sign language to the other passengers. Neither Mother nor I could understand. I went up to the attendant and said, "Good afternoon. My mother and I don't speak the language."

The woman said, "You're talking!"

"Yes, I am. I'm speaking in English but I do speak some Swedish and I also listen."

She asked, "Can you hear me?"

I said, "Yes, of course."

She said, "But how did you get on the plane?"

"I bought the tickets."

She said, "But you're speaking Swedish. Are you Swedish?"

I said, "Not only am I an African American, but so is my mother. No, we're not Swedish." We were asked to line up, then board a bus that would take us to our hotel on the Left Bank.

By the time we arrived there, the deaf people knew very well the two black ladies did not speak sign language. The hotel clerk spoke to us in French. Fortunately, my French was good enough. We were given rooms and told to return in the evening for wine before dinner, which was included in our ticket.

We had such a marvelous time in Paris that we extended our stay by a week. I rented an apartment from a woman I knew. It seemed to have a beautifully attended room, with a loft that could be seen from below. A single bed was visible, which was obviously where Mother and I would sleep.

My mother sat smiling. She didn't speak French. When the new landlady prepared to leave, Mother whispered, "Where is the toilet? It's a beautiful apartment but isn't there a toilet?"

So I asked my acquaintance where the toilet was. She walked to the living room, bent down, took a hook that that was nearly hidden there in the rug, and pulled. A large piece of the floor was raised and we saw a ladder. There at the bottom was a wonderful large kitchen and a beautiful bathroom.

My mother said, "Now, now, baby, you've got one on me."

28

My mother's gifts of courage to me were both large and small. The latter are woven so subtly into the fabric of my psyche that I can hardly distinguish where she stops and I begin.

The large lessons are highlighted in my memory like Technicolor stars in a midnight sky.

I met loves and lost loves. I dared to travel to Africa to allow my son to finish high school in Cairo, Egypt. I lived with a South African freedom fighter whom I met when he was at United Nations petitioning for an end to apartheid in South Africa.

We both tried to make our relationship firm and sturdy. For a while our attempts were successful. When our attempts failed, I took my son to Ghana and the freedom fighter returned to southern Africa. Guy entered the University of Ghana.

My mother wrote to me and said, "Airplanes leave here every day for Africa. If you need me, I will

"This last husband of Mom's was my favorite. We were made for each other. He had never had a daughter and I had not known a father's care, advice, and protection since my teens."

(Vivian Baxter with her husband, Nollege Wilburn)

come." Her love and support encouraged me to dare to live my life with pizzazz.

I met men, some of whom I loved and trusted. When the last lover proved to be unfaithful, I was devastated. I believed our relationship had been made in heaven, with thousands of baby angels dancing on the head of a pin. The dismay that flooded my heart caused me to move from my home in Ghana to North Carolina.

I was offered a lifetime professorship at Wake Forest University as Reynolds Professor of American Studies. I thanked the administration and accepted the invitation. I would teach for one year and if I liked it, I would teach a second year. I found after teaching one year that I had misunderstood my calling.

I had thought that I was a writer who could teach. I found to my surprise that I was actually a teacher who could write. I settled in at Wake Forest to be a teacher for the rest of my life.

My mother complimented me on my decision and said I would do wonders.

I sat in the beauty salon having my hair cut and curled. The general conversation was typical of black beauty salons. "Are you crazy?" asked a group of black women.

One woman said in a complaining voice, "I don't think anything is wrong with old folks having sex. It is just that the idea is sad."

"Old folks look sad having sex? Who told you that lie?"

"What's wrong with you?"

Another woman waited until the clamor had subsided and asked sweetly, "What do you think your mommy and daddy did after you were born? They stopped doing the do?"

The whiner reacted petulantly. "You don't have to be nasty." The statement brought howls of derision.

"Girl, you are sick."

"Get a grip."

Then the oldest woman in the room said, "Honey, tired don't mean lazy, and every goodbye ain't gone."

I was reminded of my mother when she was seventy-four. She lived in Stockton, California, with my fourth stepfather, whom she called her greatest love. He was recovering from a mild stroke. Her telephone voice clearly told me how upset she was. "Baby. Baby, I've waited as long as I could before bothering you. But things have gone on too long. Much too long."

I made my voice just as soft as hers had been hard. "Mom, what's the matter?"

Although I now lived in North Carolina, I felt as close as the telephone, airlines, and credit cards allowed me to be.

"It's your papa. If you don't talk to him, I'm going to put his butt out; out of this house. I'll put his butt on the street."

This last husband of Mom's was my favorite. We were made for each other. He had never had a daughter and I had not known a father's care, advice, and protection since my teens.

"What did Papa do, Mom? What is he doing?"

"Nothing. Nothing. That's it. He's not doing a damn thing."

"But, Mom, his stroke."

"I know. He thinks that if he has sex, he'll bring on another stroke. The doctor already told him that isn't true. And I got so mad when he said he might die having sex, I told him there's no better way to go."

That was funny, but I knew better than to laugh.

"What can I do, Mom? Really?"

"Yes, you can do something. You talk to him. He'll listen to you. Either you talk to him or I'll put him out on the street. I'm a woman; I'm not a damn rock."

I knew that voice very well. I knew that she had reached her level of frustration. She was ready to act.

"Okay, Mom. I don't know what I will say, but I'll talk to Papa."

"You'd better do it soon, then."

"Mom, you leave the house at five thirty this evening and I'll telephone Papa after you've gone. Calm your heart, Mom. I'll do my best."

"Okay, baby. Bye. I'll talk to you tomorrow."

She was not happy, but at least she had calmed down. I pondered throughout the day what I could possibly say. At six o'clock California time I telephoned.

"Hi, Papa. How are you?"

"Hey, baby. How you doing?" He was happy to hear my voice.

"Fine, Papa. Please let me speak to Mom."

"Oh, baby, she left here 'bout a half hour ago. Gone over to her cousin's."

"Well, Papa, I'm worried about her and her appetite. She didn't eat today, did she?"

"Yes, she did. Cooked crab cakes and a slaw and asparagus. We ate it all."

"Well, she's not drinking, is she?"

"She had a beer with me, and you can bet she's got a Dewar's White Label in her hand right now."

"But, Papa, something must be wrong. I mean, is she playing music, cards, and things?"

"We played *Take 6* all day on this music system you sent us, and I know she's playing dominoes over there with your cousin."

"Well, Papa, you seem to think her appetite is strong?"

"Oh, yeah, baby, your momma's got a good appetite."

"That's true, Papa." I lowered my voice. "All her appetites are strong. Papa, please excuse me, but I'm the only one to speak to you. It's true her love appetite is strong, too, and, Papa, please excuse me, but if you don't take care of her in that department, she will starve to death, Papa." I heard him cough, sputter, and clear his throat.

"Please excuse me, Papa, but someone is at my door. I love you, Papa."

There was a very weak "Bye, baby."

My face was burning. I made a drink for myself. I had done the best I could, and I hoped it would work.

The next morning, about 7 A.M. California time, my mother's voice gave me the result.

"Hi, darling, Mother's baby. You are the sweetest girl in the world. Mother just adores you." She cooed and crooned, and I laughed for her pleasure.

Parents who tell their offspring that sex is an act performed only for procreation do everyone a serious disservice. With absolute distress, I must say that my mom died four years after that incident, but she remains my ideal. Now in my eighties, I plan to continue to be like her when I reach my nineties, and beyond, if I'm lucky.

Mother gave her children all she had to give, but I was never as lonely as Bailey for her presence. He always was the most precious person to me in my life and I had him. He, on the other hand, ached for her and all that the memory of her contained. He was five when we were sent away, and his young years were already filled with the sounds of music and laughter and the smack of her kisses.

The whirr of wheels and the honking of horns, the screech of sirens outside the house, the voices calling and shouting, were all in his hearing memory. Naturally, the empty roads and the barely furnished quiet rooms of Stamps could not satisfy him. He could not make Arkansas fit his soul's desolation. But back with her in California, too, it was never quite enough. When he gazed at Mother, his glance was complex: Worship shared space with disappointment.

She was here, right now, where he could see her, but she had not been there when he needed her so desperately.

He began flirting with heroin at eighteen. He brushed off my concern. "I can handle it," he said. He thought his high intellect could protect him from addiction. He was wrong. He left the merchant marine and San Francisco and began living in a drug-filled area nearby.

A dreadful premonition visited me. I thought I would be called and told that he was dead. The possibility nearly took my legs away. I began to stumble and even to stutter.

I found him in a shoot-up house in East Oakland. I had followed a suspicious trail until I came to an old house with broken windows. The front door was guarded by two gaunt, grim men in dirty clothes.

One asked, "What do you want?"

I said, "I've come for my brother." There was neither fear nor hesitation in my voice.

The man nearest the door asked, "Are you the heat?"

I said, "No." I raised my voice. "I am Bailey Johnson's sister and I've come here for him." The man heard my determination, then stepped away from the door as if choreographed. I entered the stench and gloom. Immediately I realized I had never been in a place like that. When my eyes adjusted to the dimness, I saw Bailey sitting on a sofa bed, leaning back against the wall. I sat down beside him.

"Bail, I've come here to get you. Let's go," I said.

He raised up a little. "My, this is not your role. I am the big brother. You don't come down and get me."

I said, "Somebody has to do it. If not me, who?"

"Nobody. This is my life. I want you to go home."

"I don't want to leave you here. Next thing you'll be in jail and who wants to go to jail?"

"Your mother said jail was made for people, not horses. Jail does not frighten me."

I saw I was losing the conversation, if in fact I had not already lost it altogether. I put more urgency in my voice. "Bailey, I don't want to leave you here. Anything can happen."

He said, "And it probably will. You get up and go home to your son. I'm not doing too many bad things. I'm a fence. I sell hot goods to people who want bargains. I'm not hurting anybody but myself. Get up and go now. I don't want these people to see too much of you."

182

I started to cry.

He said, "For God's sake, don't whine. You can't change me, but you can change you. Get on and go home." He stood up. "Now."

I joined him.

"I'll take you to your car," he said. "Let's go."

As usual, I obeyed. Outside on the steps he spoke to the two doormen. Bailey said, "This is my sister and she won't be back."

The men murmured and their behavior told me that Bailey was in charge.

At the car he said, "Stop worrying about me. Your mother understands that this is my life and I will live it as I see fit."

Later, when I spoke to Mother about Bailey, she said, "Bailey has his own life. He's never forgiven me for sending you all to Arkansas. I'm sorry that he can't let that go. But I did the best I knew to do and I can't undo history."

Bailey met a girl who looked like Mother. She was pretty and, more important, she had a snappy personality. She spoke loudly and laughed often. His marriage to Eunice was his lifesaver. They moved to Hawaii and he was able to live a life so clean and normal that upon looking at him, it was hard to believe he had ever been a drug addict.

The couple took up tennis seriously and hiking as a pastime. But Bailey's marriage was cut short by Eunice's unexpected death. My brother lost his tenuous hold on sanity. He went to the funeral wearing his tennis whites and carrying two tennis rackets. He went to the open casket and laid one racket over her body. Within a week, Bailey had disappeared again into the greedy maw of the drug world.

Vivian gave me all she had to give me. Her son Bailey had disappointed her. She thought that since his father had not accepted the chance to teach, to guide his manhood, she would do it. She didn't consider that as a woman she could not possibly be a man, that as a mother she was unable to be a father.

She ladled the syrup of motherhood love on him. She told him that although he was a Johnson, the most important genes in his body were those he inherited from his mother. He was a Baxter.

Bailey adored her but he was unable to always forgive her for sending him away. He could not banish the memory of the lonely Arkansas years, when he never felt at home. He was five years old when we reached the country roads and quiet, nearly bare rooms of Arkansas.

Perhaps his young years had held on to the sound

of loud laughter and music and arguments, which he had heard in his infancy.

Grandmother's store and even the loud singing in the Sunday church could not drown out his mother's voice.

"[Bailey] saw his mother, his home, and then all his lonely birthdays were gone. His nights when scary things made noise under the bed were forgotten."

29

The telephone call had brought me across the country to my mother's hospital bed. Although she was a pale, ashen color and her eyes didn't want to stay focused, she smiled to see me.

With a little voice she said, "Baby, I knew you would come."

I kissed her dry lips and said, "I'm here. Everything will be okay." Although I didn't believe that, I said it because that was the only thing to say.

Her smile was even but she tried to show that she also believed me. After a short visit, during which I did all the talking, I went to confer with her doctors. Their prognosis was unpromising. Mother's ailment was lung cancer along with emphysema and they estimated that she might have at most three months to live.

I knew she would live better in North Carolina because I would be at her side and would make her as comfortable as possible. When I asked her, 'Would you come to North Carolina and let me take care of you?" she brightened up and whispered, "Yes."

Rosa Faye, my brother's firstborn, agreed to travel with Mother to Winston-Salem. I returned to North Carolina to prepare. I had a large, bright room painted a pale pink, complemented by colorful floral draperies. The room was cheerful and welcoming and I hung paintings and family photographs.

When the car arrived bringing my mother and Rosa, Mother was so weak she was unable to walk or even stand. The driver picked her up and brought her into the house carrying her in his arms. I embraced her and led the driver to her room. Mother sat on the side of the bed and looked around me, then gave me a wide smile. She said, "Baby, it's beautiful. You decorated for me, didn't you?"

I said, "Yes. How did you know? Do you smell the paint?"

"Yes, a little, but that doesn't bother me. You painted it pink because you know I love pink. I am going to get well here," she said.

Her statement was not weak with hopefulness; it was strong with certainty. The doctors who were awaiting her arrival entered her room and closed the door. We waited nervously for their findings. The doctors joined me at my kitchen table while Rosa made Mother comfortable. They said, "We read her California doctors' records and we need to examine her at our hospital. Bring her in tomorrow."

The North Carolina doctors discontinued chemotherapy and instead prescribed a therapy of radiology. Mother's spirits rose every day. After a week she called me to her room and asked me to help her out of her gown.

"You've always been fond of art. Now look at your mother." The radiologists had painted her bust and back with bright red and yellow paint. "Do I remind you of Picasso?" she asked.

I was happy to laugh with her and to know that although she was not healed, she had chosen to be better. After two months, one of the physicians, Dr. Imamura, said there was no explanation for her recovery. Salt-and-pepper hair began to grow on her bald head. She had enough appetite to ask for substantial food and even to offer to cook it for herself. Within six months she gained weight and strength. She began entertaining friends and went with me to church.

With Mother's steady improvement, I was encouraged to return to my work, which was lecturing around the country. Mother asked if I would send for her closest friend, Aunt Area, and I said yes.

She asked, "Isn't it time for you to do the work that you have to do?"

I said, "Yes."

She said, "Then you'd better do it."

My two housekeepers were massive women of height and girth. Ms. Knowles, who lived in, was six feet two and weighed 275 pounds. Mrs. Sterling, who came daily, was five ten and about two hundred pounds. Mother treated them as if they were her little girls. They loved it and behaved accordingly.

Aunt Area arrived and right away I wished I had sent for her earlier. She and my mother laughed and giggled and my house was wonderful to be in, totally free of the fear and apprehension that had filled it before. Mother was comfortable and happy. Each time I packed to leave, I noticed a kind of holiday spirit in the air. My mother would hold my hand and kiss my cheeks.

"Oh baby, Mother is going to miss you. You have a good time and come back soon. Mother needs you," she would say.

The car taking me to the airport would be hardly out of the driveway when my mother would call all my employees from the office and the house and inform them that she and Aunt Area were taking them to lunch at a local seafood restaurant. She had booked a limo for her and Aunt Area. "Get ready. Let's go and let's eat."

30

An invitation arrived that stunned and thrilled me. England's University of Exeter invited me to come and teach for three weeks in their hallowed halls as distinguished visiting professor. I thanked the administrator but said no, I couldn't leave North Carolina, because my mother was gravely ill.

When Vivian Baxter heard that I had rejected the invitation, she called me to her room. "Go," she whispered. "Go. Show them you spell your name W-O-M-A-N. I'll be here when you get back!"

I left North Carolina and began lecturing at the Exeter campus. I telephoned each day to check on my mother's recovery.

One day Guy called and told me, "Mom, Grandmother is not pleased with Aunt Area."

"Why not?"

Guy said, "Aunt Area wants to put the sides up around Grandmother's bed, and she disagrees. She

*"You've been a hard worker—white, black, Asian, and Latino
women ship out of the San Francisco port because of you.
You have been a shipfitter, a nurse, a real estate broker, and a barber.
Many men and—if my memory serves me right—a few women
risked their lives to love you. There has never been anyone
greater than you."*

wants to spend her time sitting up on the side of the bed."

I telephoned Mom. "Mother?"

She whispered, "Yes, baby."

"Would you like me to send Aunt Area back to California?"

She nearly shouted, "Yes."

I told her I would send her back the next day.

She hummed her gratitude.

I asked my secretary to have a large check cut and to deliver it to Aunt Area the next day at one o'clock.

I telephoned Auntie at 12:50 P.M. "Auntie, thank you for coming to see after Mother. I appreciate that."

She said, "She's my sister. I had to do it."

"Now Auntie, it's time for you to go home. She needs to live her life on her own terms. I'm told that you don't want to allow her to sit on the side of her bed."

"That's right. She is sick. She could fall off the bed."

I said, "Auntie, she is dying of lung cancer. So what if she wants to sit on the side of her bed? I'm going to give you something to thank you for coming to see about her."

"You can't pay me for looking after my sister."

At that moment, my secretary entered the room

and laid the check down in front of Aunt Area. She read it and melted. "Oh, Maya, baby, thank you. I love you and I love your mother. I will go back to California and keep my sister in my prayers."

Two days later, I decided to leave Exeter for home. I was picked up at the Greensboro, North Carolina, airport and taken to my mother's hospital room.

Vivian Baxter was in a coma. I spoke to her anyway. Her hand lay in mine without movement.

The next day I hired three women to sit with her in shifts of eight hours each.

"You don't have to nurse her. There are nurses here to do that. I only want you to hold her hand. If you have to go to the toilet, let someone else hold her hand until you return. I want her to have human contact as long as she is alive."

On the third day after I returned, I went to visit Mother. I took her hand and said, "I've been told some people need to be given permission to leave. I don't know if you are waiting, but I can say you may have done all you came here to do.

"You've been a hard worker—white, black, Asian, and Latino women ship out of the San Francisco port because of you. You have been a shipfitter, a nurse, a real estate broker, and a barber. Many men and—if my memory serves me right—a few women risked their lives to love you. You were a terrible mother of small children, but there has never been anyone greater than you as a mother of a young adult."

She squeezed my hand twice.

I kissed her fingers and gave them back to the woman sitting beside her bed. Then I went home.

I awakened at dawn and raced downstairs in my pajamas. I drove to the hospital and doubled-parked my car. I didn't wait for the elevators. I ran up the stairs to her floor.

The nurse said, "She just left."

I looked at my mother's lifeless form and thought about her passion and wit. I knew she deserved a daughter who loved her and had a good memory, and she got one.

Resolution No. **92-0739**

STOCKTON CITY COUNCIL

WHEREAS, pursuant to City Council Policy No. 400-1, "Naming of City Parks, and Buildings and Facilities Located Within Parks," the Stockton Metropolitan Park and Recreation Commission recommends that the three (3) proposed park sites be named as described below; now, therefore,

BE IT RESOLVED BY THE COUNCIL OF THE CITY OF STOCKTON, AS FOLLOWS:

1.   That the 11-acre community park site within the Brookside subdivision is hereby named HAROLD "HAL" NELSON PARK.

2.   That the 5-acre neighborhood park site in the Phase I, A. G. Spanos subdivision is hereby named VIVIAN "LADY B" BAXTER PARK.

3.   That the 6-acre neighborhood park site in the River Estates subdivision is hereby named JOHN PERI PARK.

PASSED, APPROVED and ADOPTED _____ DEC 14 1992 _____.

JOAN DARRAH, Mayor
of the City of Stockton

ATTEST:

FRANCES HONG, City Clerk
of the City of Stockton

c:\wp51\agd\rso\NamePark.1

CITY ATTY
REVIEW
DATE DEC 1 1 1992

92-0739

Like her daughter, "Lady B" was noted as a great storyteller and served as founder and president of the Stockton Black Women of Humanity, which provided scholarships to black high school students. She was also an active member of a Masonic order, a past chairwoman of Concerned Women for Political Action, and a board member of the United Way, San Joaquin County Blind Center, Women's Center of Stockton, and Board of Directors of Gemini, Inc.

The City of Stockton takes pride and pleasure in naming this park site today in memory of Vivian "Lady B" Baxter, a woman who devoted her life to help anyone in need.

NAMING OF PARK SITE, MARCH 4, 1995

ACKNOWLEDGMENTS

*To all parents who have dared to raise daughters and sons
with love, laughter, and prayers.
Who have stumbled and fallen, and yet arisen
and gone on to be successful mothers and fathers.*

*And to all whom I have kept
under a mother's watchful eye:
Oprah, Stephanie Johnson, Lydia Stuckey,
Valerie Simpson, Bettie Clay, Ceda Floyd,
Dinky Weber, Jacqui Sales, and others,
you know who you are.*

I thank God, and I thank you.